Remembering and Forgetting
in the Age of Technology

TEACHING AND LEARNING IN HIGHER EDUCATION
James M. Lang, Series Editor

A list of titles in this series appears at the end of this volume.

REMEMBERING AND FORGETTING IN THE AGE OF TECHNOLOGY

Teaching, Learning, and the Science of Memory in a Wired World

Michelle D. Miller

West Virginia University Press
Morgantown

For my mother, Dr. Darla Ferris Miller

CONTENTS

—

—

MACHINES, MEMORY, AND LEARNING

—

Our minds are made of memories, and today, those memories have competition.

Where we once depended on human memory—our own, other people's, the collective knowledge of a society passed down orally and in books—we now turn to digital records. Computers ranging from tiny wearables to vast AI-driven networks are what we rely on to remember, to remind, and to reminisce. For most of us, these machines have seamlessly integrated themselves into every corner of our lives. We are at a point in history where it's impossible to talk about human memory without also talking about the digital memory mechanisms that run alongside our own.

And make no mistake, we do need to be talking about memory. For one, there's simply more to know today than there ever has been before; name almost any subject area or professional specialization, and there's a vast and exponentially growing knowledge base that goes along with it. There are also greater rewards now for people who've cracked the code for acquiring and using knowledge, who know how to deliberately practice and improve on what they know and what they know how to do, who can learn deeply but also efficiently. There are greater rewards for people who know how to manage cognitive resources and direct them productively, despite the intrusions of a frantic and hyperconnected world. These expert mind-managers will have the greatest competitive edge, the most options, and the best chance of living well in the world we now inhabit.

Memory is important for everyone, but for those of us who teach, it's absolutely critical. I say this in spite of the bad reputation that the topic has within education circles. Everybody has now heard the adage that a real education is about learning to think, not about memorizing facts; while this may be true, it hinges on a dichotomy that contemporary researchers know to be a false one. Committing information to memory isn't the be-all and end-all of learning, but it is assuredly one important part of learning. Far from competing with thinking skills, having a well-established base of knowledge actually supports the ability to reason in a given topic area. And fortunately, with new research-based, superefficient memory techniques, there's really no reason why learners can't do both.

Clearly, people who care about education need to care about memory. As far as who ought to care about education— well, today, that should be all of us. We now live in a time when quality education is the difference between succeeding wildly and falling tragically behind, both for individuals and for whole societies. This doesn't just refer to the transfer of knowledge that takes place in formal educational settings, although that is a big part of it. It also means the ways in which people continue their educations, through self-teaching and dipping in and out of just-in-time, informal learning throughout their lives.

To promote this kind of lifelong learning, we can tap into the techniques developed for higher education—in other words, the kind of teaching that's geared to adults. There's recently been an explosion of interest in advancing and refining college-level pedagogy, and developments in the field show no signs of slowing down. Techniques for making higher learning more accessible, more inclusive, and simply more effective now fill scholarly journals, periodicals like *The Chronicle of Higher Education*, books, and entire book series (like the one that this volume is a part of).

This interest in creating great college pedagogy is a major development, and one with real potential for positive social impacts. I've taught college classes for around a quarter century now, with most of these courses being offered at a public institution serving students from across the social and economic spectrum. Over and over, I have seen for myself the incredible promise of what college can do when it's working as it should. Getting that degree, and more importantly the skills and knowledge that go along with it, radically expands the range of options for what students can do with their lives. I can only imagine what will happen as more people all over the world get the same chance at these options that my own students do, whether it's through obtaining formal degrees, taking advantage of online classes, or learning on their own. This is world-changing stuff, and it's exhilarating to get to be a part of it.

Today is also a great time to be a teacher because of radical improvements in the advice given out to people who are looking to build or improve their teaching practices. The wisdom dispensed to generations of instructors used to be heavily based in the philosophical stance and personal experience of whoever was dispensing it, and not a whole lot more. Now, guidance for teachers is increasingly grounded in good-quality empirical research in the learning sciences—an umbrella term that includes psychology as well as related areas like education and neuroscience. Research in these fields has reached a real critical mass in recent years, revealing not just *what* works in education but also *why* these techniques work. There are now well-developed, precisely articulated theories of how we think and remember that go well beyond the simplistic models that used to populate textbooks for teachers. Take, for example, the three-box theory of memory, the one that shows information passing through sensory, short-term, and long-term memory as if your memories were widgets on an assembly line. Today's researchers know that there are many more components of memory and many more influences on what we remember than that. They've turned their findings into more nuanced, and more practically useful theories. And more than ever before, faculty across disciplines are using advice derived from these theories to devise more compelling, more effective learning experiences.

In addition to giving a much clearer picture of how memory works in the context of learning, these models also let us make better predictions about what will happen when new factors such as cell phone cameras or search engines are thrown into the mix. Pundits may editorialize about whether smartphones are killing our inborn ability to remember experiences, or whether Google is somehow making us stupid, but good theories let us put these opinions to the test. Theories point us toward the underlying dynamics we should zero in on as we try to predict the likely impacts of all these new factors. Put another way, if we start by grounding ourselves in the fundamental principles of how memory works, those principles can act as a filter that lets us sort plausible claims from wildly improbable ones.

Technology and Psychology Go Back a Long Way

Concerns about cognitive impacts of technology may seem as though they were touched off for the first time by the spread of cheap, addictive, infinitely portable computing devices—the smartphones, smart watches, tablets, and so on that are the highly visible hallmark of our time. But although it is true that the links between technology and human cognition have reached a new level of practical importance, the idea that we should look at one in light of the other is not new. Technology and the study of the mind have a long and complicated relationship, one that goes all the way back to the inception of the field where I've spent my academic career, cognitive psychology.

Cognitive psychology focuses on the ways in which people take in, process, and use information. These mental processes are elusive, imperceptible, and maddeningly hard to pin down, even compared to other constructs that research psychologists might study. So when the creators of the field were hashing out their first tentative ideas of how human beings process information, they needed a way to talk about these invisible things going on, rapidly and mostly unconsciously, within the mind. This was a problem, because back in the 1950s and 1960s when cognitive psychology was first getting started, research psychologists studiously avoided the whole subject of mental processes, considering these to be a minefield of intangibles that could never be pinned down through empirical research techniques. Determined to maintain their legitimacy as real scientists, they refused to engage with all the invisible stuff going on in the head, preferring to concentrate on outward behaviors that they could see, measure, and quantify. Today it seems a little bizarre that behavioral scientists would deliberately ignore the mental machinations that lead to visible-and-countable behaviors in the first place. But for the first psychologists, focusing on invisible constructs such as memory was a slippery slope down which the whole science could easily tumble, down into the realm of mere armchair speculation.

Enter the computer metaphor. Despite the fact that at the time, computers were exotic things well outside most people's experience, likening mental processes to algorithms brought cognition into the realm of subjects fit for scientific study. Computers made information processing tangible, something that happened predictably and systematically through the workings of the programs they were running. Especially in the case of memory, computers also gave us a model for what it means to take in, store, and retrieve information, providing a way to think about these processes as well as the terminology for talking about it.

This new conception of minds-as-computers was a turning point for our science, demonstrating that even though thought processes were (and still are) impossible to observe directly, they could be studied quite systematically. The metaphor was the toehold we cognitive psychologists needed to lift ourselves up into the realm of real, credible, quantitatively based science, and for that we are forever grateful. Even today, the analogy remains part of our disciplinary DNA, coloring and shading the ways in which cognitive psychologists look at the mind.

However, the link between human memory and digital memory has now turned from a useful metaphor into a literal relationship, with each one shaping and influencing the other. And the relationship isn't always a friendly one. Cultural commenters, and some scientists as well, are now asking whether technologies invented to help us are instead undermining our ability to remember and even to think. Now that computers have moved from being ultra-technical pieces of equipment housed in research facilities to being personal belongings that rattle around in our pockets along with loose change and car keys, the interplay between their digital brains and our biological brains has moved from a theoretical question to a practical one.

On the one hand, this relationship could be described as a sort of benign symbiosis.[1] Human beings bring digital memory devices into existence, and then they populate those devices with knowledge. In turn, humans depend on those digital devices to help us cope with the demands that life throws at us. One major way devices do this is by shoring up our own fragile memories and extending our ability to use what we know. Digital memory plays this supporting role beautifully; it holds more, stays more consistent over time, and works more predictably than human memory ever could. It's possible to exploit this complementary relationship quite strategically by using computers to do things our brains don't do well, which in turn frees those brains up to do all the things they *do* manage well. In this ideal scenario of brain-machine symbiosis, technology opens up untold potential for human beings to reach new heights of reasoning, productivity, and personal achievement.

On the other hand, though, is the nagging question of over-reliance, such that the technologies that were meant to enhance our own inborn cognitive abilities end up eroding them. Like midsections turned soft because of cushy desk jobs, are our modern minds weakened by an excess of support? Or if not weakened exactly, are they subtly reshaped by the expectation that technology will always be there to help backstop our failures of memory? How often are people simply not bothering to create their own memories, knowing in the back of their minds that they can always fall back on external aids?

Even more unsettling is the question of distraction, which has moved from an unfortunate side effect to a feature deliberately designed into apps, social media, and into mobile devices themselves. Distraction has pernicious effects on memory, and even when we know this fact on an intellectual level, we're terrible at predicting when and how badly a lack of focus is going to affect our ability to take in and store information.

These now-pressing concerns shape the questions at the core of this book: Does technology enhance memory, and by extension, all of our other cognitive capabilities that depend on memory? Or does technology erode memory, making us dependent and getting in the way of creating new memories? Does it do some combination of all of these things, depending on the setting and activity? And importantly—what does this mean for teaching and learning? How much does it matter that today's young adults grew up totally immersed in digital media and computing, and how much should we change our teaching (if at all) to take this into account?

There are multiple perspectives on, and multiple answers to all of these questions. However, I have no intention of throwing up my hands and calling it a draw. There may be a wide spectrum of thought on these issues, and certainly plenty of nuance to consider, and yet there are some firm, defensible statements that we can make based on the science to date. These include intriguing links between knowledge and thinking ability. There are also the clear connections between distraction and forgetting, which have played out in numerous research projects on the ways in which devices can interfere with learning. Finally, there are examples of ways in which technology has been used to amplify and advance cognitive processes—whether by enhancing memory in the context of learning or in other aspects of everyday life. Technology does not do one simple thing to memory or to any other cognitive process, for that matter. But it does have a number of systematic effects that we can draw conclusions about based on the research to date, interpreted through the lens of theories that we've developed.

Structure of This Book

The ideas above are what I will be making a case for throughout the book, starting with a critical look at the assumptions about technology that we, as a culture, bring to the table. These assumptions go surprisingly deep, and can be found in one form or another throughout the history of how our culture has received new technologies; they're reflected today in what we write and say about our tech. After taking a critical look at these assumptions about what technology actually does and doesn't do to us, we'll go into the reasons why we remember and forget what we do, based on the principles of memory that have coalesced from of hundreds of studies on the subject. From the theory, we'll turn to practical questions: Is memory still relevant to teaching and learning, and if so, what does research say about the best ways to build and improve it? And in order to make this happen, we also have to consider the question of attention, which is needed in order to form any new memories and which is increasingly divided in our click-driven world.

Next, we'll turn to the question of how all of these cognitive processes interact with the kind of mobile technology that travels around with us, starting with the iconic device of our age: the smartphone. Even during their short time in existence, smartphones have generated a flurry of new research on how they affect thinking and memory, and this research has practical applications that can help us make decisions about how to manage phones in our classrooms and other areas of life where memory is important. This topic leads to the next issue, one that has sparked an astonishing amount of polarized debate in education circles: laptops and the controversy over whether note-taking by hand is superior to note-taking via keyboard.

In the concluding chapter, I'll return to big-picture questions involving computing and memory, and what these mean for all kinds of learning, broadly construed. Is there really a generational divide in how we think and remember, and if so, how consequential is this divide for learning? How might our attitudes about and approaches to memory continue to evolve in a world where so much information can be retrieved online? And lastly, what can we all do to promote learning in this world of ubiquitous, sometimes intrusive, and rapidly evolving computing and communications technologies?

To get at these kinds of questions throughout the book, I'll be tapping into research from my academic background as a cognitive psychologist. This means I'll be citing studies that are mostly, but not always, based on experiments done in laboratories, or sometimes, done through the use of surveys. While these methods aren't a perfect way to get at what goes on in the mind, we in the field have made a lot of progress in refining them in recent years. And so I'd argue that these tactics are still the best option if we want to get a handle on why we remember, forget, and think in the ways that we do. I will also bring in some cognitive neuroscience, meaning research that looks at the same kinds of questions, but gets at them by examining physical structures and processes in the brain. It's important to keep in mind that these kinds of studies aren't necessarily more illuminating or more reliable than their laboratory counterparts. But they can add new insights, when they are designed and executed using the same kinds of quality standards—and who's not at least a little excited to know more about what's physically going on in the brain when we do things like remember and think?

However, there is going to be more to my approach than just reviewing the scholarly literature. I'll also be drawing on another experience I've been fortunate to have in my career: talking directly to "traditional-aged"[2] college students themselves about the role of technology in their lives and what they think it means for learning. Too much of the discussion about technology's effects on young people is conducted *about* them, not *with* them, and I think this is a shame, for two reasons. For one, it leads to a prescriptive approach to technology that's heavy on scare tactics and light on useful advice. You'd think that after decades of risible attempts at intergenerational fearmongering—think *Reefer Madness* or Your Brain On Drugs—adults would have learned to take a more subtle and open-ended approach. A glance at anti-tech op-eds, however, suggests that we have not. For another, staying stuck in the mode of lecture-from-on-high causes those of us in an older demographic to miss out on some of the best ideas out there for how to manage the down sides of ubiquitous technology. After all, who could be better at finding the best hacks than people who've handled these challenges since they were old enough to hold an iPad?

I'm fortunate to have a better window than most middle-aged people do into what traditional-aged, Generation-Z college students really think about technology. This is not just because part of my job is teaching college courses;

it is because of a specific course that I've gotten to teach over the last ten years or so, a seminar called *Technology, Mind, and Brain: Using Psychology to Thrive in a Wired World*. In this course, we read research articles and develop projects, as one typically would in a seminar. More importantly though, this class presents one of the only opportunities my students—and I—get for in-depth, no-judgment, cross-generational discussions about what they really think about the technology that defines their demographic. Their viewpoints are varied, as you might expect. But on the whole, they are sophisticated, thoughtful, and couldn't be further from the stereotype of glued-to-the-phone digital natives in thrall to every kind of online diversion.

The last source of insight for this book is my fellow faculty. I'm fortunate to be able to tap into the experience I've had, through my research and also my work in university-level course redesign, working with instructors across disciplines to reflect on and refine their teaching. Especially in the years since my last book (*Minds Online: Teaching Effectively with Technology*), I've been able to be a part of many, many discussions with highly accomplished faculty, watching and listening as they wrestle with the biggest challenges of their profession. I can say this group has an awe-inspiring level of devotion to the mission of helping students advance intellectually, professionally, and personally. Their wisdom is woven throughout these pages.

Who This Book Is For

More than anything else, I wrote this book for my fellow faculty, people who create and deliver courses in colleges and universities. Increasingly, college instructors have begun to see themselves as being in the business of changing minds and brains, and are eager to see the latest research on how these change processes work. If some or all of your career portfolio consists of teaching, and if you're curious about the processes that underlie learning, this book will fit that bill. Today, teaching in higher education is also far more of a team effort than it has historically been, drawing on the talents of people who may not be in front of students each day but who make contributions of all kinds outside of the classroom. Instructional designers, coaches and tutors, academic skills instructors, student success program directors—all of these professionals now work to help push the quality of courses forward and support students as they progress through those courses. If your professional portfolio looks like this, you'll also find a lot that you can use in this book.

There's another important group for whom I wrote this book. These are people who don't have teaching listed as any part of their job descriptions, but who are deeply engaged in helping other people develop their own skills, knowledge, and insights. More than ever, these kinds of development efforts are critical to progress, both the progress of individual careers and of our human society as a whole. I've come to believe that in our contemporary, knowledge-and-technology-focused era, it is not only lifelong learning that provides the key to success. It is also lifelong *teaching*.

Especially as the concept of college-level teaching has evolved from a narrow focus on presenting information to a more sophisticated emphasis on designing and orchestrating learning environments, the broad applicability of teaching techniques has become more obvious. Great teaching is, after all, the art and science of clear explanation, of persuasion, inspiration, and moving people to action, of selecting the best information and getting it across in ways that stick and stay in memory. Health care, marketing, customer service, even designing good web sites all involve skills that are ready and waiting in the teacher's toolkit. Especially any time these tools involve making something memorable for your listener, user, or customer, this book will show you how to accomplish that goal in a contemporary environment awash in technology.

And lastly, I wrote this book for anyone with a keen interest in memory. This interest might grow out of practical concerns—coping with aging, gaining an edge in hobbies or work, or just the hope of being a little less forgetful as one moves through life. Or it could be because you share the same lifelong fascination with memory that I do. It has, after all, been something that has intrigued storytellers and puzzled philosophers for ages—how it is that we write our life story in our own minds, hour after hour, saving some moments forever and letting the rest slip into oblivion.

Questions about memory go to the heart of who we are and how we see the world. And so, I still experience a sense of wonder every time that I sit down to write about it, even after so many years studying the subject. It brings to mind the dying words of *Blade Runner's* war android Roy Batty, as he contemplates the end of all that he remembers: "I've seen things you people wouldn't believe. Attack ships on fire off the shoulder of Orion. I watched C-beams glitter in the dark near the Tannhäuser Gate. All those moments will be lost in time, like tears in rain. Time to die." Memory is, in a sense, existence. And in that way, to know memory, and to gain just a little more control over what we do and don't remember, is to get that much closer to making the most of our time on earth.

What to Expect from This Book

This book will explore memory from both the practical and the abstract side, with the aim of ferreting out the specific ways in which our contemporary technology alters this key aspect of our psychology. Besides the big overarching questions I listed above, there are those that tie directly to our teaching practices: Should we remove laptops from learning environments? Do learners remember less when they can fall back on technology? How can new technologies be used to boost learning and amplify what we're able to do with our brains alone? To help make this book as useful as possible as you apply it to your own teaching, I've provided a summary at the end of each chapter, listing key principles and the pieces of advice that flow from those principles.

I should also say a few words about what this book is not. Although it's heavily influenced by my background as an ed-tech researcher, it's not an instruction manual on how to incorporate technology into our courses. Nor is it a textbook packed with comprehensive reviews of different general theoretical frameworks for learning; there won't be discussion questions, exercises to do, or checklists. It is not a general guide on how to teach, although it will help elevate your teaching practice in ways that add to what you can learn from all the other great guidebooks out there.[3] And finally, the book isn't, and indeed could never be, the last word on this subject. Even though the study of memory has already generated a massive research literature, new studies and new perspectives are added every day. Although it seems like technology can't get any more sophisticated or more pervasive than it already is, the next revolutionary change is really just one product launch away. Because of this, nothing I say is going to be timeless, nor definitive.

Here's what I want to deliver to you by the end of this book. If you are in a traditional teaching job, especially if it's focused on teaching adults, you will come away with the best understanding that current science has to offer on how to craft learning experiences that jibe with the ways in which people learn. You will be able to make highly informed decisions about policies and practices that have been the subject of fierce, polarized, and often completely inconclusive debates. These informed decisions will balance the positive aspects of what technology can do in a classroom with the risks and downsides. You will also be able to give your students good advice about how to manage their own cognitive capacities in a wired world. Should they engage in tech fasts? Should they be vigilant about certain kinds of distractions, and how should they follow through on tech management plans? Which of the dire warnings blared out about technology should they pay attention to, and which can they safely ignore? With the right information, we teachers can offer the kind of informed and effective leadership that our students look to us to provide.

Besides advice, I promise that you'll come away with a deeper understanding of the reasoning behind the advice. Especially if we're going to be ready for whatever the next technological wave turns out to be, it's not enough just to have a list of do's and don'ts—we need to dig down into the inner workings of the mind that underlie why we remember and forget what we do. Attention, too, is an area where myths and misunderstandings thrive, and it's another area where this book can offer an understanding based on the current science. For those readers who are lifelong learners and lifelong teachers outside of traditional higher education, or who want to use this book to learn how to coexist better with their own technology—these foundations are what will allow you to do that. Research will expand, computing will change, but the bedrock principles of why we remember and forget are going to last. It's that beautiful heart of the science of memory that I want to share with you in this book.

More than anything, I promise that this book will offer good explanations and research-tested perspectives in an area where there hasn't been much middle ground between contentious clickbait articles and opaque technical research. With this, I hope to help us all plot a better way forward as we navigate lives saturated with more technology and more to know than any human beings have ever experienced before.

—

CHAPTER 1

WHAT TECHNOLOGY DOES TO US (AND FOR US)

—

Taking a Critical Look at Common Narratives

Consider what these commenters have had to say about the impact of rapid technological advancements on the human mind:

> "The current explosion of digital technology not only is changing the way we live and communicate but also is rapidly and profoundly altering our brains. . . . Because of the current technological revolution, our brains are evolving right now—at a speed like never before."—Gary Small and Gigi Vorgan, "Meet your iBrain"[1]

"The power of the unaided mind is highly overrated. Without external aids, memory, thought, and reasoning are all constrained. But human intelligence is highly flexible and adaptive, superb at inventing procedures and objects that overcome its own limits. The real powers come from devising external aids that enhance cognitive abilities."—Don Norman, *Things that Make Us Smart: Defending Human Attributes in the Age of the Machine*[2]

"Technology can potentially improve education, dramatically widen access, and promote greater human creativity and well-being."—Gene Tracy, "How Technology Helps Our Memories"[3]

"I am convinced the devil lives in our phones and is wreaking havoc on our children."—Athena Chavarria,[4] parent quoted in a *New York Times* article titled "A dark consensus about screens and kids begins to emerge in Silicon Valley"

Once you start looking into the question of how technology affects memory—and by extension, learning—you enter a thicket of opinion and commentary, much of it heavy in its pronouncements about what tech can do *for* us, or is already doing *to* us. The impacts of various digital innovations are now an evergreen source of material for news feeds, blogs, and other various forms of editorializing. This has created an arms race of sorts about who can make the most extreme claims about how these play out in our lives, our minds, and even within our brains. Many of the more out-there claims are of the alarmist variety. Others allude to the wonders of technology and its unlimited potential to transform for the better all the ways that we get through life, from shopping to socializing to learning.

So out of all the contradictory opinions like the above examples, which are actually in line with the science of how we think and remember? Are *any* of them?

One of the reasons I set out to write this book was to address exactly this kind of polarized discourse about the ways in which living in the contemporary world is affecting our minds. Throughout our culture, the voices of caution, in particular, are beginning to meld into a chorus of increasingly familiar complaints. They go like this: Technology distracts us and distorts thinking. It blunts and dilutes our natural abilities to remember, to record, to reason. It's a cognitive crutch that makes us lazy.

What's the support for ideas like these? Some are based purely on opinion or personal anecdote, but increasingly, critics point to research from psychology and neuroscience to make the case for the cognitive dangers of digital devices. Whether the research in question consists of findings from high-tech, cutting-edge studies of the brain, or data coming out of more traditional laboratory experiments run by research psychologists, there is supposedly ample scientific reason to look on our personal technologies with suspicion.

And many of us do look on these things with, if not outright suspicion, ambivalence. When the Pew Research organization[5] queried a group of technology experts and health specialists about the changes in human well-being that might happen because of advances in personal computing technology, the responses reflected a characteristic mix of worry and hope. On the one hand, most of Pew's experts predicted that technology's impacts would be generally positive. They cited outcomes such the option to connect socially with people all over the world and the ability to access information on everything from science to health to safety. This is nothing to sneeze at, given that these kinds of resources are now available to a wider and more diverse swath of the world's population than ever before in human history.

However, the pro-technology vote wasn't exactly a landslide, with only 47% endorsing this positive viewpoint. 32% said the impacts would likely be bad, and a minority—21%—said that there wouldn't be much change at all in well-being specifically due to technology. Especially telling were the specific kinds of harm that the anti-technology camp cited when they predicted that tech would send well-being on a downward spiral. Of the themes that Pew pulled out of the responses, four out of five were psychological. "Digital distrust" was one, characterized by deepening divisions among people as a function of having their worldviews and beliefs pitted against each other on social media. Similarly, "digital duress" reflects a decline in social interactions and face-to-face relational skills that some experts believe is happening as a function of moving so much of our social lives online. This kind of distress is exacerbated by advertisers' constant push to make people feel less satisfied with their possessions, lifestyles, and life circumstances. Social media also encourages unhealthy comparisons by constantly exposing users to the intimate but sanitized-and-idealized details of how other people live. Lastly, straight-up internet addiction was another, not-surprising psychological hazard that made the list of potential ills.

Notably, though, there was one threat at the very top of this list: declines in cognitive capabilities. In other words, according to Pew's experts, the constant connectivity and inherent distractions of contemporary technology are doing harm to our ability to think, to pay attention, and most importantly for the purpose of this book, to remember.

Could this be true? Could using mobile computing devices—cellphones, tablets, laptops—impede formation of memories? And if so, would that impediment be transitory, something that dissipates when you put the device down? Or, would it be something more ominous: a global degradation of our ability to retain information? This is the kind of risk that we hear the direst warnings about. It is a sobering thought indeed, that even when our devices are off and out of sight, they have rewired us in some permanent way. Under these circumstances, even a digital detox might not be enough to restore us to our prior state of mental clarity. If this viewpoint is correct, the damage is real, and for most of us that damage is already done.

Hold up, another group of skeptics would say. The idea that tech is toxic to your mental faculties is a fairly recent one, but there's a familiar ring to the warnings. Could it be that similar dire predictions have blared out for the technologies that came before our mobile devices, and the technologies before them, going back through the twentieth century and perhaps even before? Well, yes, the pro-technology side would say, because today's technology critiques have all the hallmarks of the fallacy known as moral panic.

Is Technology Provoking Moral Panic, Once Again?

"New forms of media have always caused moral panics: the printing press, newspapers, paperbacks and television were all once denounced as threats to their consumers' brainpower and moral fiber," cognitive psychologist Steven Pinker wrote in a 2010[6] *New York Times* opinion piece. Sociologist Stanley Cohen coined the term long ago to talk about the demonization of certain strains of 1960s youth culture, but the idea seems surprisingly timely even today. As one 1990s-era commentator put it, moral panic is "characterized by a wave of public concern, anxiety, and fervor about something, usually perceived as a threat to society. The distinguishing factors are a level of interest totally out of proportion to the real importance of the subject, some individuals building personal careers from the pursuit and magnification of the issue, and the replacement of reasoned debate with witchhunts and hysteria."[7]

"Witchhunt" is probably too strong a term for antitechnology sentiment in our culture; to my mind, this sentiment seems to have settled into a low-level ambient hum of complaint, criticism, and concern. Nor has the sentiment triggered a serious or organized movement toward stopping the march of tech into daily life. But even so, the subject seems to take up an unusual amount of space in the public consciousness, considering the actual proportions of the issues at stake.

Take as an example the issue of screen time among young kids. Anything connected to child-rearing in our culture tends to elicit powerful emotions, and people are quick to conclude that today's parents are somehow dropping the ball. Combine that with worries about new technology and the whole topic might unleash a torrent of judgment that's largely disconnected from empirical evidence. This is usually what happens when I ask my own students to discuss technology's influence on kids. Although most are traditional-aged students without firsthand parenting experience, invariably some will speak up about a perceived epidemic of parents obliviously checked out while kids run wild online. Those who've worked as restaurant servers frequently heap scorn on parents they've seen giving children smartphones or tablets to pacify them during a meal.

This perception that parents these days are irresponsibly

shoving devices into kids' hands just to give themselves a break doesn't jibe with the evidence, though. In another set of Pew Research Center surveys, large majorities of parents stated that they imposed limits on screen time and set up other kinds of restrictions and safeguards.[8] Most also said that technology made it harder to parent children compared to 20 years ago, and expressed a wide variety of related concerns, such as the idea that smartphones will damage kids' social skills, academic progress, and even creativity.

In forming these attitudes, parents are likely picking up on guidelines issued by authoritative bodies such as the American Academy of Pediatrics, which over the years has issued strict and specific limits on how many minutes a day should be allowable for children of various ages. But parents might be surprised to know that the evidence base behind these guidelines is somewhat thin. For example, one study of a representative sample of nearly 20,000 American parents sought to test whether preschoolers with higher screen time scored lower on some accepted measures of children's mental health.[9] The correlations that did exist were very small, on an order of magnitude that would be invisible in normal everyday circumstances. Some actually ran in the *opposite* direction from what you'd assume, so that for some demographic subgroups of kids, well-being actually went up as daily screen time increased.

Of course, the study's findings aren't an argument for a total free-for-all. The authors stress that factors such as the quality of the activities themselves—a variable that wasn't measured in the study—probably matter a great deal. It also couldn't fully account for the opportunity cost of screen time, meaning tradeoffs with other, healthy activities that kids might otherwise be doing, if they weren't on an electronic device. But the study does illustrate how easy it is to seize on a highly visible incursion of technology and assume that it's creating all kinds of serious problems.

I'd argue that the topic of screen time also does elicit the disproportionate scrutiny that's typical of moral panic. Compare the energy unleashed by this one question—how much tech is okay at what ages—with others that affect young children today. There are the known and substantial effects of childhood poverty. There's the immense and completely preventable loss of human potential that happens because of grossly underfunded schools. Or consider climate disruption and armed conflict, both of which are clear and present threats to the world's children. Seen in this perspective, the worry, parent-shaming, and indignation around screen time seem outsized indeed.

What about the other component of moral panic, the part about profiting from amping up public concern? This one is a tougher call, because it's hard to distinguish warnings that come from a place of authentic worry from those that emanate from less pure motivations. The rise of influencer culture, in which attention equals clicks equals money, also makes it hard to say where the intangible benefits of a message leave off and tangible ones begin.

I don't think that people who speak out in favor of less screen time for kids are only in it for the notoriety, and there is a real possibility that future studies will uncover hazards that the research to date has not. However, commercial products connected to technology distrust in general do present a more clear-cut case of profiteering. The rise of goods and services designed around the ideal of a lower-tech, distraction-free lifestyle is hard to miss; I know that my own feeds are teeming with ads for things I can buy to help clear my mind of techno-fog. Bullet journals and gorgeously designed paper notebooks invite me to dream of the mindfully composed, handwritten to-do lists that will turn my life into a Zen vision of organized minimalism. E-writers that do everything *except* connect to the Internet promise an unplugged experience for authors yearning to write without pings, notifications, and the siren call of social media.[10] In the case of writers for whom a screen of any kind is too much, there's now a mini-revival of typewriters going on.[11]

Delightfully, for fans of irony at least, there's even technology you can buy to rein in your other technology. You can install an app like Freedom to block yourself from accessing social media, news, and other usual suspects across all of your various devices. Another app, Forest, polices how often and when you unlock your phone, growing a virtual tree while you leave your phone closed for a preset amount of time. If you cave in and unlock it before your time is up? The tree dies. It's not subtle, but it does grab your attention.

These tech-control apps are not a bad thing; I'm a devoted user myself of a freeware product called SelfControl that applies an impossible-to-evade block[12] on sites that you specify ahead of time, for up to 24 hours at a time. Anti-tech tech tools do make it much easier to set yourself up for success as you resolve to spend less time in mindless scrolling. The kind of "precommitment" strategy they support, where you lock future-you into a virtuous course of action, is something that is supported by plenty of research[13] on intentional behavior change. Beneficial or not, though, most of these are products created to generate money, often by channeling peoples' worries about distraction into sales. It follows that the more upset people are about incursions of technology into their lives, the better those profits will be—exactly the kind of perverse incentive called out by the moral panic concept.

Classroom technology policies, site-blocking apps, dire warnings about the mental impacts of rapid technological change: All of this is timely, today's-front-page kind of stuff. And yet, history does seem to be repeating itself, nearly verbatim. As I observed in my own book[14] published in 2014, there is a startling amount of overlap between today's technology critiques and the things said in mass media about the incursions of radio into the lives of families many years ago. Writing about this parallel, the communications scholar Evelyn Ellerman pointed out that "dozens of scholarly books were written, from the late 1920s into the 1940s, studying the ways in which the new technology was reshaping personal relationships, the structure of the family, the literacy of children, and the ability of people to think critically and express themselves clearly. We have only to pass by the shelves of any bookstore to see this whole process repeating itself with respect to the Internet."[15]

There is something about new inventions, especially those that spread quickly and deeply into our everyday lives, that sets off a particular blend of revulsion, fascination, and worry. But this dynamic should raise red flags as we seek to dig below the headlines and do our own critical reflection on the issues. Yesterday's threat is today's quaint piece of nostalgia, and I for one don't want to look back on anything I've said about a technology and have it look laughably histrionic by the standards of some future day. Nor do I want complicated truths to be swept away in a tidal wave of premature consensus about things that "everybody knows" are true of contemporary technology.

The idea that technology would be bad for thinking in general, and memory in particular, has circulated through so much of our popular culture that it's taken for granted. But consider its polar opposite: the school of thought that holds that technology isn't just neutral for thinking, but is actually a solid positive.

Can Technology Enhance Cognitive Abilities?

Maybe technology can enhance cognitive ability, but how? The claim makes sense when we look at computing technology as existing along a continuum with all the other objects that human beings invent to extend our power and accomplish our goals. This is the stance Gavriel Salomon and David Perkins took in a 2013 article titled "Do technologies make us smarter? Intellectual amplification with, of, and through technology." As they observe:

> The impulse to make what you do not have runs deep in the human mind. Children design implements such as cranes made of sticks, string, and house keys, and transform pairs of socks into balls to play with . . . From the dawn of civilization, people have created physical and symbolic devices that help them do what they cannot accomplish through bare flesh and bone: tools, instruments, machines, writing systems, mathematics, and on and on. Such products of human invention extend both our physical and our intellectual reach.[16]

Salomon and Perkins extend the analogy between cognitive tools and physical ones, pointing out that just as attempting to do some physical tasks with bare hands is fruitless, so is trying to do some kinds of cognitive work with "bare brains." In that sense, digital applications help us do things that our brains don't handle well. This doesn't just widen the range of tasks that we're able to do competently—it frees up capacity to focus more on things our brains *do* handle well.

Take spreadsheets. You might be thinking, "please," but as those of us who predate Excel can attest, these maligned applications are a fantastic replacement for the tedious and error-prone work of recording information in ledgers and logbooks. Spreadsheets keep your information organized neatly and legibly, and they perform repetitive functions—calculating percentages in columns, filling in dates, assigning grades—accurately and instantaneously. You can copy and share them, either prefilled or as an empty framework for someone else to populate with whatever data they like. Since neither copying neatly nor accurately performing the same calculations over and over are strong suits of human cognition, I count that as a big win for technology.

In theory, the time saved in recording and tracking data can be funneled into the kinds of thinking in which humans do excel (sorry). So for example, the time I save in having to calculate the percentage of points earned by each student in a class can be put into picking more challenging readings or creating an interesting activity for them to do. In that way, the technology may not be making me smarter, but it's allowing me to do a lot more with the smarts I have.

According to Salomon and Perkins, there are additional, more subtle impacts of software such as spreadsheets. These tools can change our mastery of the skills associated with the software, producing intellectual impacts that persist even when we aren't actively using that tool any more. So for example, my spreadsheet app might change the ways in which I think about organizing quantitative information, helping me develop a more sophisticated conceptual understanding of how things like formulae work, thereby producing an improvement in my cognitive abilities.[17] Conversely, using spreadsheets could erode my ability to perform calculations in my head, something we'd categorize as a cognitive loss. Or it might just predispose me to visualize data in particular ways, a cognitive change that's essentially neutral.

There is one last kind of impact, one that sits at the top

of the hierarchy proposed by Salomon and Perkins. The existence of calculation tools like spreadsheets doesn't just extend my abilities and it doesn't just change my own mind. It could change *all* of our minds as far as how we think about data and calculation in general. In other words: Spreadsheets change how we think about numbers. So did calculators, and so did abaci. Word processing changes how we think about language. So does the existence of a written alphabet.[18] In sum: The unique properties and affordances of the things that we invent *all* color, shape, and eventually transform the things we think about.

The notion that our tools make us smarter is not some loopy fringe philosophy that sprang up as pushback against mainstream anti-tech critics. It has been around for years, well before contemporary worries about smartphones and laptops took over the discussion. In the time since its inception, there has developed a body of interesting and often-surprising research evidence for the positive impacts of technology. The educational psychologist Susanne Lajoie likens digital tools to cognitive amplifiers or even a type of prosthetics that extend the mind's reach, putting complex concepts within our grasp and accelerating the acquisition of content knowledge. Well-designed learning programs, Lajoie argues, can do things like help students develop scientific reasoning by engaging them in simulated hypothesis testing. In some ways these virtual science exercises are even better than the real thing, because particular aspects of the reasoning process can be isolated and reinforced. Learning can also be scaffolded with extra resources so that students don't get stuck when they are missing a piece of factual knowledge or particular vocabulary term.[19]

The eminent cognitive psychologist Raymond Nickerson also proposes an amplification metaphor for technology's impacts, pointing out that since antiquity, people have invented tools that extend cognitive capabilities and let us do a lot more with the brains we have. These tools for thinking include computing devices that well predate even the vacuum-tube machines we think of as primitive today: slide rules, gauging rods, mechanical calculators capable of temporarily storing and moving around small amounts of information.

Most critically for the questions at the heart of this book, Nickerson also observes that amplification of memory has been a focus of human technological innovation going back centuries or more, if we count items such as almanacs and encyclopedias. Like the Internet today, these served as repositories for more knowledge than any mind could hold, and provided users with ways to retrieve what they needed when they needed it.[20] Clearly, people have wanted to supplant their memories for a long time, reflecting both how important memory is to us and also how puny our memory abilities are in their natural, unaided state. What this also shows is just how well-suited technology, especially contemporary digital computing, is for buttressing and amplifying human memory.

The concept of technology as a springboard to human thriving was summarized best of all by Don Norman, a cognitive scientist, design visionary, and the author of one of the quotes at the top of this chapter.

[O]ver the years, the human brain has remained much the same. Human intelligence has certainly not diminished. True, we no longer learn how to memorize vast amounts of material. We no longer need to be completely proficient at arithmetic, for calculators—present as dedicated devices or on almost every computer or phone—take care of that task for us. But does that make us stupid? Does the fact that I can no longer remember my own phone number indicate my growing feebleness? No, on the contrary, it unleashes the mind from the petty tyranny of tending to the trivial and allows it to concentrate on the important and the critical.

Reliance on technology is a benefit to humanity. With technology, the brain gets neither better nor worse. Instead, it is the task that changes. Human plus machine is more powerful than either human or machine alone.[21]

Does Using Technology Rewire the Brain?

Besides advocating for the net positive impacts of technology, Norman's quote calls into question another assumption that tends to go along with an anti-technology stance: the notion of deep physical changes to the brain wrought by computing. The idea that human brains have been fundamentally altered in recent times sounds ominous enough, especially if you think these changes are for the worse. It also resonates with the perception many of us have that the world is changing at an overwhelming pace, and we humans along with it.

However, this is another claim that sounds a little silly to most psychologists.[22] Within the field, our disciplinary lens tends to direct our focus toward the underlying mental architecture that humans have in common, much of which reflects the evolutionary forces that shaped that architecture.

If we're being literal about it, there is no way that natural selection could have acted so quickly on human brains to physically change them in the time since computers were invented. But even in a looser, nonliteral sense, there are limits to how deeply the brain can be remodeled by *any* experience, be it an experience with technology or anything else. As the cognitive psychologist Steven Pinker puts it, "Yes, every time we learn a fact or skill the wiring of the brain changes; it's not as if the information is stored in the pancreas. But the existence of neural plasticity does not mean the brain is a blob of clay pounded into shape by experience. Experience does not revamp the basic information-processing capacities of the brain."[23]

Psychologists like Pinker might be skeptical of the re-wiring trope solely based on its face validity. But isn't there other evidence that technology changes us at a neural level?

This question gets especially interesting when you take a close look at the study that's frequently referenced in support of technology's special powers to change the brain. This project, executed by a team of UCLA brain research-ers, carried the intriguing title "Your Brain on Google: Patterns of Cerebral Activation during Internet Searching."[24] Researchers asked 24 volunteers to complete a simulated search task while in a functional magnetic resonance (fMRI) scanner. Half of those volunteers were "net-naive," meaning that they reported minimal experience with using the web or search engines. (Keep in mind that this research took place before 2009, when such individuals still existed outside of hunter-gatherer societies and hardcore minimalist circles.) The other half of the volunteers were dubbed "net-savvy," meaning that they reported using the web habitually in their everyday lives. While in the scanner, both groups searched for information in two ways, one using a simulation that was much like a traditional paper book, and another with a simulation of searching via web browser. The distribution of neural activity[25] was compared across both tasks and across both groups, with the goal of determining whether the vol-unteers' brains responded differently to internet versus text searching, and whether that disparity was different based on the level of web browsing experience that volunteers had (net-naive versus net-savvy).

The short story of the project's findings is yes to both questions. More areas of the brain fired up in response to the simulated internet search task relative to the plain-text one, especially regions involved in decision-making, visual processing, and attention. However, this was *only* true for people with prior web browsing experience, that is, the net-savvy group. Those with limited prior experience with the web didn't exhibit this same pattern of enhanced activation in response to the simulated web browsing task. However, after just about five hours of web experience, the brains of net-naive volunteers also started to show that fired-up pattern associated specifically with searching for information via the web.[26]

From this set of findings, it certainly looks as though using a computer creates lasting physical change in the brain. But let's dig deeper into the limitations of this particular study. Yes, 24 research participants is a fairly small sample,[27] but it's not too unusual in the realm of fMRI studies, which are usually designed to involve a fairly low number of individuals given the time and money involved in running people through the scanner. More importantly, there is this problem: To this day, researchers don't know what it means to have more extensive activation associated with a task, at least not in a big-picture sense. We still can't answer the basic question of what it means when one group is using more brain capacity overall, or a more extensive set of circuits and structures to do a task. Are the people in that group doing the task less efficiently? Are they more engaged as they do the task? Are they processing information in a way that is qualitatively different, compared to those exhibiting less extensive activation? These problems have been discussed at length among neuroscientists but are still essentially unsolved, which makes it hard to characterize exactly what was different about the experienced Web users in this particular study.

Even more importantly, there is the matter of the age of these two groups of participants. Both groups were composed of older adults, averaging 66 years old in the net-naive and 62 in the net-savvy groups, and it's worth noting that this study was originally published in a source (the *American Journal of Geriatric Psychiatry)* that is clearly focused on the psychology of older people. The research group was transparent about the focus on older adults, and there's nothing inherently flawed about such a design choice. Pragmatically speaking, it also made it possible to assemble a net-naive group (something the researchers admit[28] was a bit of a challenge as they were setting up the study). All of this makes sense, but we have to keep in mind that the brains of older and younger individuals are simply different, especially when it comes to memory, attention, and new learning.[29] This means there are some fairly major limitations on how far we ought to generalize the findings across age groups.

But generalize many have. The findings regarding technology-caused brain changes have most pointedly been extrapolated to the brains of adolescents and young adults—the people who are, after all, the main focus of the lion's share of articles about the dangers of technology. The researchers in charge of the UCLA web browsing study themselves characterize the study as "exploratory,"[30] offering the caveat that they can't definitively demonstrate cause and effect given the correlational study design. And as is customary at the end of such studies, the researchers plead for caution in how the findings are interpreted. And yet, these cautions were tossed out the window as the findings made their way out into short research summaries and popular press articles.[31]

Oddly, the study's results were cited not only in favor of the creepy-rewiring idea, but also its mirror image, the notion that interacting with the net is a brain-building positive. As the lead author Gary Small said in a press release about the work, "A simple, everyday task like searching the Web appears to enhance brain circuitry in older adults, demonstrating that our brains are sensitive and can continue to learn as we grow older,"[32] clearly characterizing brain change as a good thing. As the original article says as well, "Our present results are encouraging that emerging computerized technologies designed to improve cognitive abilities and brain function may have physiologic effects and potential benefits for middle-aged and older adults . . . our findings point to an association between routine internet searching and neural circuitry activation in middle-aged and older adults. Further study will elucidate both the potential positive and negative influences of these technologies on the aging brain and the extent to which they may engage important cognitive circuits controlling decision making and complex reasoning."

Even beyond the unsettled issue of whether these brain impacts are positive, negative, or neutral is the question of how unique the changes associated with technology really are. There's no question among modern neuroscientists that the brain is plastic, meaning that it physically reshapes itself throughout our lifespans. These changes are frequently the result of experiences: memories we form, compelling emotions we have, and new things we learn how to do. Viewed in this light then, it's not surprising that our brains would change as a function of engaging in tech-driven activities, especially those that elicit emotions, require us to develop new skills, or that simply take up a lot of our waking hours. Flip the question around, and it would be weird if our brains were somehow selectively impervious to this particular class of experiences.

While the rewiring and reshaping of brain tissue might sound unsettling, it's also something that happens to an even greater degree in response to other, nondigital technologies that we engage with.[33] A perfect example is reading. Written words are, after all, a technology of sorts, and processing them requires major renovation of the brain.[34] Humans come prewired to process language as an auditory experience, so in order to decode language using our eyes, we have to sprout new connections between these language areas (located mostly in the left temporal lobe of the brain, near your left ear) and areas devoted to visual processing (the occipital lobes, located at the back of the head). These changes are deep, lasting, and consequential, yet in this day and age nobody writes ominous opinion pieces about the ways in which books are reprogramming us.

Even something mundane like learning to drive a car is going to change your brain, and if you were to repeat the UCLA study with drivers and nondrivers, it's likely that you'd pick up a similar pattern of results.[35] The brains of experienced drivers would show a heightened response within new neural pathways they built to handle this engrossing new activity; nondrivers would start without any such specialized neural activity but would acquire it in short order after intensive practice with the machinery.

So what should we, as teachers and critical thinkers about technology, take away from this line of research? It doesn't make sense to simply dismiss the findings out of hand, although the study's limitations—the number and type of individuals in the sample, interpretation of what it means to see more brain activation among experienced participants—are substantial ones. Mainly, I think that this highly publicized work spotlights the engaging nature of the technology we use to explore new information, and therefore, its power to entice us into spending copious amounts of neurally impactful time using it. It is that ability, and not some unique power over our brain matter, that allows technology to change us.

The research also raises another question, one that's useful to have in mind as we explore the landscape of research, theory, and opinion on the subject: Why, if the evidence for it is so thin, does the rewiring notion get such traction? Perhaps it comes down to the same forces that feed into all moral panic: worries about large-scale social transformation, coupled with intergenerational tensions and a good dose of suspicion about new things that have entered our lives. Headlines claiming that something new "changes everything" are catnip for readers, resulting in immense pressure on writers, editors, and pundits to spotlight research that fits that idea while simultaneously suppressing anything that contradicts the narrative.[36]

Why does this matter? Besides being hard to support with good evidence, the rewiring idea can undermine our teaching. One way it does this is by exaggerating differences among individuals based on their relative familiarity with technology. This exaggeration gives rise to an educational philosophy in which the younger individuals being taught—be they kindergartners, adolescents, or traditional-college-aged people—are a fundamentally different sort of being than you, the teacher. How much common ground could there be, really, between people whose brains have been drastically reshaped, compared to your own? In this sense, teaching becomes a matter of reaching across a cognitive gulf, picking and choosing modalities that will reach learners who are very different than ourselves. Good perspective-taking skills are essential to great teaching, to be sure.

Staying aware of the dynamics that exaggerate technology's power, and counterbalancing them whenever we can, is an important part of our own critical inquiry as educators. If we really do care about thinking, memory, and learning, and the cognitive processes that support all of those things, we are going to need to look underneath the headlines and get into the details of the actual research. It's not that dramatic impacts of technology *never* happen; there really are some stunning findings in the area, and the rest of this book's chapters will draw on those remarkable studies, details and all. But to see the true importance of the research, we need to first self-inoculate a bit against the trendiness, panic, and hype that attach themselves to topics of technology and social change. It's especially needed in education, which has long had a problem with fads based on shaky interpretations of existing science.[37]

Better Ways to Look at Technology and the Mind

There's one last caution I want to add, and it has to do with a kind of othering we do when we talk about the technological inventions of humankind. So many of our discussions and debates seem to be predicated on the unspoken idea that digital technology is something done *to* us, rather than something we humans gladly and eagerly do to ourselves.

Smartphones, social media, notifications, and search engines didn't come from outer space, even though you might think so given the way they're talked about. Rather, these things all sprang from our keenly felt human desires. There is the desire to be connected to each other. To have access to the information that our memories can't hold. To share the images and sounds that move us so deeply as human beings. To be the first to know the important things happening in the world, while they are happening. To chase our interests to our heart's content, find answers to questions, and have an ever-changing feed of content that is completely personalized and thoroughly relevant. In a word, our technology is us.

Or, you could say that our digital innovations are a mirror, reflecting back our own essence as a species—the things we like, the things we want, the things we most love to do. Perhaps the even more apt analogy is that of a magnifying mirror—something that intensifies, exaggerates, and occasionally distorts the features of our human character. Granted, the picture isn't always a pretty one, but it arises directly from who we really are.

Technology is reflective, and cyclical, and it's anything but alien to our human minds. As Raymond Nickerson describes it: "The relationship between technology and cognition is one of dependency that goes both ways. There would be little in the way of technology in the absence of cognition. And cognition would be greatly handicapped if all its technological aids were suddenly to disappear. Technology is a product of cognition and its production is a cyclic, self-perpetuating process. Cognition invents technology, the technology invented amplifies the ability of cognition to invent additional technology that amplifies further the ability of cognition . . . and so it goes."[38]

Nickerson's calm and optimistic take on the relationship between minds and machines may not jibe with all of the research we'll consider in this book. But this kind of reasoned, evidence-grounded mindset is what we will need if we are going to help our students make technology a healthy and positive force in their lives. Students look to us for that kind of leadership, and we're well positioned to offer it to them.

It's also a mindset that helps us discern the right reasons for including, or excluding, technology from our classrooms. Teaching today means making that choice; even those of us who want to opt out of adding technology of our own can't avoid it, as we still have to decide what to do about the devices that students carry in to class, and we still have to consider how our course material plays out in the context of a decidedly technological world. When we can avoid fallacies like moral panic and magical thinking as part of these technology choices, we're better placed to take advantage of the good while sidestepping the bad.

CHAPTER SUMMARY

- The idea that technology degrades cognitive capabilities is a widespread one, but it is not clearly supported by research. Some scholars have made the opposite argument, that technology enhances and helps us make the most of our cognitive capabilities.
- Some cautions about technology may also be rooted in moral panic, a fallacy marked by concerns out of proportion to actual danger, coupled with a profit motive. In this way, some of the common narratives about technology echo much earlier ones, such as worries about radio and television.
- Technically, computers and mobile devices do reshape the brain through frequent use. However, other

activities—notably, reading—do as well, and so this concern is one that we can comfortably set aside.

- Generations are more similar than different when it comes to basic cognitive functions such as memory and attention. It is unlikely that human cognitive capabilities have been changed at a fundamental level as a result of innovations such as mobile devices.

- Some scholars have advocated for the idea that technology strengthens our cognitive capabilities, pointing out that we can do a lot more with technological aids than we can with "bare brains." Offloading routine processes onto computers can free us up to concentrate on higher-level reasoning and even creative thought.

- The relationship between technology and the human psyche is reciprocal and cyclical. We develop tools to shore up our weaker capabilities and to meet core human needs, and in turn, technological developments change how we think.

TEACHING TAKE-AWAYS

- Avoid recirculating the kind of simplistic, alarmist narratives about technology that dominate headlines in the popular press. Present students with reasoned, evidence-based viewpoints, and encourage them to apply critical thinking as they develop their own views and practices relating to technology.

- Look for opportunities to develop students' thinking in new ways through technology. For example, statistics programs can encourage students to explore data and practice interpreting statistical tests in a way that hand calculation or simple spreadsheets cannot

- Avoid assuming that your younger students think fundamentally differently than you do because they've grown up surrounded by mobile devices and the Internet. Some are probably even less comfortable than you are with these things.

- Consider the way that you use software in your own teaching, for example, to handle routine communications, create materials, or track grades. You might be able to strategically reroute more of your own capacity into higher-level, high-impact pursuits like giving better feedback or designing creative new learning activities.

—

WHY WE REMEMBER, WHY WE FORGET

—

"Clara Peller!"

This what I blurted out to my husband, Rick, during one of our many discussions about growing up back in the day.

I was feeling pretty pleased with myself, having nailed the actual full name of the person who was briefly famous as the *"where's the beef?"* lady on a set of strangely compelling 1980s TV ads for the Wendy's fast food chain. This feeling lasted only until Rick reminded me of how just a few minutes before, I had drawn a total blank on the name of the current pope.

In my defense, my memory is great for a lot of other things:

I know how to hold my yarn to do a long-tail cast-on when I'm starting a knitting project. I know that bolo ties are the official neckwear of my home state of Arizona, and have special legal standing as appropriate attire for official state functions. I remember in terrifying detail how I got stung by a whole nest of enraged wasps when I was five. There's a decent amount of knowledge left in my brain about psycholinguistics, even though I acquired almost all of that when I was studying memory and language back in grad school. I also have a fine verbatim recollection of an elegantly structured joke involving a motorcycle cop and a woman who's knitting while driving.[1]

But then again, here are some of the things I have thoroughly forgotten:

Whether I turned off the iron when I left for the office this morning. Basically everything taught in the Western Civilization class I took my freshman semester (I believe we discussed Rome, but that's about it). Most of the names of the students who were in my classes last year. The scientific name for wasps. The exact point in my notes where I left off in last week's Language and Cognition class lecture. From which source I learned that appealing set of facts about Arizona's official neckwear (was it a friend? A book? Wikipedia?). And, frequently, where I parked my car.

You've got your own list of memory wins and memory fails, and when you look at all of those, the pattern is probably not all that different than my own.

Memory is a bit of a paradox. It's at once orderly and systematic, governed by some reasonably simple principles that cognitive psychologists have managed to get a fairly good handle on. At the same time, it's often undependable and a bit chaotic, retaining some items permanently and remaining stubbornly impervious to others. Sometimes the things it's impervious to are those we desperately wish we could remember. Sometimes what memory serves up, preserved in perfect detail, are things we wish we could forget.

Some of our memories can vanish over time; in other cases, they last just fine but are distorted or even completely wrong. Sometimes memories elude us, but only temporarily: Picture yourself in the midst of a conversation about the

Guardians of the Galaxy movies, when you realize you can't remember the name of the guy who played Dr. Strange.[2] It sits there on the tip of your tongue, evading all attempt at capture, then pops randomly into mind long after you've given up and moved on.

All of these quirks make it clear that remembering isn't just a process of recording what happens around you then replaying it all back later on. Memory is recording of a sort, but the idea that we store information in any way resembling what digital storage devices do is simply incorrect. And yet, it's an idea that many people believe—that memory is a recording capability in the head that takes in information in some kind of all-or-nothing, undifferentiated fashion. That human memory is on some level basically the same as magnetic tape, a laptop hard drive, or the video app on our phones.

This wrong assumption speaks to one of many strange-but-true facts about human memory: Even though we all live in our memories every waking (and dreaming) moment of every day, the intuitions we develop about memory tend to be wrong. This tendency is on full display in an ambitious study conducted by cognitive psychologist Dan Simons and his research team.[3] They carried out a large-scale phone survey of over a thousand individuals systematically sampled from the general United States population (i.e., not college freshmen in a psychology course), with the goal of finding out what people thought about basic principles of memory. In particular, they wanted to pinpoint discrepancies between what survey respondents believed and mainstream scientific understanding of memory. To do this, the researchers presented 16 statements to their survey respondents, asking whether the statements were true or false. They then posed the same questions to 16 experts in the field. These statements included:

Hypnosis is useful in helping witnesses accurately recall details of crimes. 55% of survey respondents agreed; all but one expert disagreed.

People suffering from amnesia typically cannot recall their own name or identity. 83% of survey respondents agreed; all of the experts disagreed.

People generally notice when something unexpected enters their field of view, even when they're paying attention to something else. 78% of survey respondents agreed; all but 3 experts disagreed.

They also directly queried people on whether they thought that the brain works like a recording device, through the statement "*Human memory works like a video camera, accurately recording the events we see and hear so that we can review and inspect them later.*" All of the memory experts said this idea was wrong, but more than half of the survey respondents—63%—said it was right.

This idea also came up in a study that colleagues and I conducted that focused on higher education professionals (faculty, administrators, and instructional designers)—specifically how familiar these professionals are with a number of key facts about how the mind and brain work.[4] We asked our respondents to evaluate a variation of that same statement about memory: *Human memory works much like a digital recording device or video camera in that it accurately records the events we have experienced.* Our sample scored better than Simons' did, with 74% correctly stating that the claim was false. Still though, that means that 1 in 4 people in our hyper-educated study sample, individuals with whole careers dedicated to helping people acquire knowledge, had this fundamentally flawed concept of what memory is all about.[5]

In sum, among both typical adults and people with specialized careers in higher education, memory isn't something that people just naturally have a great factual grasp of. Intuitions are incorrect, our metaphors mislead us, and even those of us who have thought about this kind of thing a lot can stand to improve. As Simons and colleagues put it: "At least for these basic properties of memory, commonsense intuitions are more likely to be wrong than right."[6]

The intuition that memory is essentially a recording, for example, is clearly at odds with a well-accepted concept known as *reconstructive memory*. According to this idea, retrieval isn't just a bit player next to the stars of the show, encoding and storage. On the contrary, it plays a surprisingly large role in what we end up remembering on any given occasion.

This concept shows up in the unsettling fact that our memories can be shaped by something as minor as a tweak to the wording of a question. The classic demonstration of this is the *misinformation effect,* something that's now in the pantheon of field-changing psychology studies that you see in just about every textbook. This phenomenon was the discovery of legendary memory researcher Elizabeth Loftus, who devised an ingenious way to quantify just how much a person's recollection could be affected through suggestion.[7] Loftus and her research team asked volunteers to witness a set of staged automobile accidents. These realistic crashes, repurposed from traffic safety films, were set up under controlled conditions, so that the researchers knew exactly how fast the cars were going.

After watching the films, volunteers were asked to give a straightforward estimate for how fast the cars were traveling. This is where Loftus's team introduced their small but ingenious twist: They varied the exact wording of the question. For some volunteers, the query was posed using terms that implied a fairly mellow event, such as *About how fast were the two cars going when they contacted each other?* Others got a version that implied a more spectacular wreck, such as *About how fast were the two cars going when they smashed into each other?*

Note that all of the research volunteers should have started out with similar memories, since they did, after all, watch an identical set of events. And yet, when asked about these memories in different ways, the volunteers gave different answers—about 9 miles per hour faster for the "smashed into" version compared with the "contacted" one.

This pattern is totally incompatible with the record-and-replay concept of memory, but fits well with a different metaphor: reassembling a set of parts, often with a few missing pieces. Without realizing it, we compensate for those missing pieces by plugging in content that doesn't actually belong in that memory. Usually this is just fine, since we're probably basing these invented parts on what's plausible for the situation. However, it leaves us vulnerable to things like leading questions, which ever-so-subtly nudge us to fill in missing memories with confabulated details that match the tenor of the questions.

The idea that memories are not replayed, but instead remade when we retrieve them, is closely aligned with another one of the fallacies queried by Simons and colleagues. This is the notion that hypnosis can tap into detailed memories hidden somewhere in the psyche. True, hypnotized people might relate far more detail about a memory when they're in this relaxed, suggestible state. However, those details probably come about through the person embellishing and elaborating during the process of reconstructing the memory, or simply because the person doing the remembering applies less stringent criteria when deciding what they think they remember.[8]

Similarly, the idea that one's whole identity could easily disappear in an episode of amnesia is easy to debunk. Much more frequently, brain injury causes the reverse kind of memory loss—the inability to create *new* memories, although old ones are spared.[9] And, people can and do easily miss all kinds of things that come into their field of view, if they're concentrating hard enough on some other aspect of their surroundings.[10]

These misconceptions matter. Simons and colleagues stress the implications for court cases; it's especially concerning that in trials that hinge on eyewitness testimony, jurors lacking a basic understanding of how memory works would be evaluating that kind of evidence. Jurors who believe in common misconceptions would be prone to do things like place too much stock in the testimony of witnesses who seem exceptionally confident in their memories, or accept testimony based what witnesses might have said under hypnosis. Nearly as bad, media might pillory a witness whose account has changed over time or shown minor discrepancies, concluding that the person was intentionally lying when they were simply displaying perfectly typical patterns of recall.

Memory misconceptions have big implications for our teaching as well. If we hew to that flawed metaphor of recording, for example, it reinforces the idea that teaching is about delivering information and learning is about being able to play it all back on demand. We might assume that just because some new piece of information was introduced during class, students would naturally notice and remember it. We might give bad study advice based on the idea that when you simply look at information long enough, it enters some kind of permanent store that students can just dip back into when exam time rolls around.

Building up an accurate conceptual understanding of why

we remember and forget what we do may be important, but it isn't easy. Not all memory theories are simple, and not all are even close to complete. The good news is that cognitive psychologists have studied this problem more than any other problem in our field, and all of this hard work has paid off. Researchers have developed a rich understanding of the inner workings of our memory systems, one that doesn't just let theorists generate after-the-fact explanations, but also reasonably accurate predictions about how these processes will play out in different situations. There's a lot that memory scientists still need to figure out, but right now, there is more than enough scholarly understanding to form a solid base for good advice about teaching and learning. We also know enough to begin to make good predictions about how technology will and won't affect learning. Or, even in cases where the facts aren't quite clear yet, there's still a basis for separating plausible possibilities from nonsense, moral panic, and hype.

So what are the biggest landmark ideas in our understanding of remembering and forgetting? Can they tell us anything about the typical patterns of what we do and don't remember? And what do they mean for teaching and learning?

Let's start with some of the classic theories.

Classic Theories of Memory

The Three-Box Model: Sensory, Short-Term, and Long-Term Memory

If you've taken an introductory psychology class, you probably at least vaguely remember a diagram that would have appeared in the unit on memory. This representation had three boxes, probably connected with arrows indicating the direction that information moved as it arrived via your senses (mainly vision and hearing). These boxes were designated "sensory memory," "short-term memory," and "long-term memory." Maybe there was a twist in terminology, and instead of short-term memory, it said working memory. Either way, that middle stop was an important one, mediating the leap from sensory impression to lasting record. There may have also been a circling arrow attached to short term memory indicating something called *rehearsal*, the process of consciously refreshing and replaying information that you're working to remember.

By way of illustration, the textbook probably explained that rehearsal is like what you do when you've been told a phone number but can't write it down, which for most people involves saying it to yourself over and over. (Today's psychology instructors have to cast about for new examples, now that you almost never have to remember phone numbers thanks to contact files and so on.) According to the theory, this rehearsal process does more than just let you temporarily hang onto a few pieces of information. It also helps make the information permanent, increasing the chances that it gets moved along the mental conveyer belt from short-term storage to long-term storage.

This model has provided a clear, concrete introduction to memory theory for legions of introductory psychology students, but here's the thing: Your mind is not a factory, and your memories are not widgets rolling off a line. This concept of memory may have been the definitive one for a few years, but it is no longer believed to be literally true by anyone in the mainstream of memory research, and even its broad parameters are now rejected by many[11] researchers. Richard Atkinson and Richard Shiffrin themselves moved on to develop other, more complex theories after developing the seminal three-box model in the late 1960s.[12]

So what's wrong with it? One problem is that we now know that, unlike a conveyor belt, the short-term memory to long-term memory route isn't a direct one. It turns out that information doesn't actually have to make a stop in short-term memory in order to become permanent. Dramatic demonstrations of this principle in action come from in-depth studies of individuals with brain injuries affecting specific aspects of memory.[13] It's possible for a focal injury, such as a stroke, to wipe out the type of short-term memory that you'd use to repeat back a list of numbers someone just told you. People with this problem might only be able to say back two or three numbers out of such a list, compared to the usual range of 5–9 that you would typically see. And yet, people with this kind of selective lesion don't display amnesia, or anything like it involving long-term memory. In fact, you'd be unlikely to notice anything unusual about them at all if you sat and engaged them in conversation, and some experience few or no impacts on their day-to-day lives despite having a major problem with short-term memory. This is totally contrary to what the conveyor-belt model predicts.

If you've ever formed a permanent memory instantly, without anything like rehearsal or deliberate practice, you've experienced for yourself the way that information can bypass short-term memory. This happens often when we encounter something personally significant, or one associated with strong emotions such as surprise or fear. We may rehearse these memories later on as we retell our stories to other people, but we don't need to do much when they are happening in order for them to make their way into more-or-less permanent storage.

This ties in to another shortcoming of the old model—it doesn't say nearly enough about the role of meaningful relationships and interpretations, although those factors have a huge impact on what we do and don't remember. When we can fit incoming material into some kind of a framework, or if it links into something we already know, it is much more likely to stick. This principle flows all the way down to how we understand spoken sentences. Decades ago, researchers theorized that when people were listening to speech, they would need to engage short-term memory pretty heavily, because spoken words are here and gone in an incredibly short period of time.[14] Listeners would need to dump words they heard into short-term storage so that they could go back and piece it all together later.

But then, researchers discovered that this isn't what we do at all. As soon as we decode a segment of speech, our language processing systems almost instantaneously fit individual words into an emerging concept of what the sentence means. Then, they throw out the record of all the individual pieces of that sentence.[15] In other words, interpretation happens right away, and when it does, the interpretation goes straight to longer-term storage, no pit stop in short term memory required.

There are plenty of other documented impacts of the importance of meaningful interpretation for memory, particularly when it comes to saving things that are personally relevant to us or that we've thought about in a way that emphasizes meaning. Besides giving yet another reason to reject the conveyor-belt, three-box metaphor, the role of meaning and interpretation are important for our teaching practices. And so, these are themes that will come up a lot in this book—that we remember things we understand, that relate to ourselves, and that we care about.

Clearly, the old-school, three-box theory isn't the best way for teachers (or anyone else) to think about memory. So if this theory is so far off base, why is it still the most commonly recognized and talked-about conceptualization? Part of it is that, although the details of the theory are almost certainly wrong, its rests on a foundational assumption that is almost certainly right: that memory isn't just one undifferentiated capacity, but is instead composed of distinct subsystems that work alongside one another in more-or-less coordinated fashion. Many researchers still believe in the distinction between memory that's immediate, conscious, and transitory, and memory that's longer-lasting and that lies dormant most of the time. Modern theorists tend to see short-term and long-term subsystems as fairly independent from one another, rather than linked in exactly the way that Atkinson and Shiffrin first envisioned. However, most of us agree that using information consciously, in the here and now, engages a different set of mechanisms than putting information into and taking information out of longer-term memory.

Let's consider in more depth exactly why it matters that teachers commonly still believe in this incorrect theory. The three-box concept may not be as pernicious as the memory-as-video-recording idea, but it is still highly problematic for our teaching. For one thing, it subtly biases us to think of memory as a container of sorts, which in turn makes us think of teaching as a straight transfer of material from teacher to student, shipping information from the container in our heads to the containers in theirs.

And indeed, leading thinkers have spent decades heaping scorn upon the container-and-transfer concept of learning. Paolo Freire, the revered Brazilian author of the classic teaching manifesto *Pedagogy of the Oppressed,* called this idea the "banking model" of education. He characterized this as a malignant metaphor that ensconces hierarchy and inequality into teaching, turning it into an exchange between an all-knowing teacher and students presumed to know basically nothing.[16] Ken Bain, the education expert who interviewed some of the most successful college teachers in the country for his book *What the Best College Teachers Do,* noted that this was also a differentiating factor between great teachers and poor ones. Discussing one of the less-successful college teachers in his study, Bain points out the passive, container-type language that professor used to talk about his students' learning. This description prominently emphasized "transmission" of knowledge, with the teacher hypothesizing that the stronger students were the ones capable of "storing away" large amounts of information and that weaker ones simply lacked the space for it in their "memory banks."[17]

Granted, it's not Atkinson and Shiffrin's fault that the container and banking notions of teaching got started in the first place; their roots run deep through our cultural concepts of teacher-student hierarchies and what learning is really about. Nor were Atkinson and Shiffrin explicitly trying to offer advice to teachers when they put the model together—on the contrary, they were mainly trying to find a way to make sense of the patterns that they saw in data generated by highly controlled laboratory tasks. However, when we fail to challenge their outdated theory, we are acquiescing to the model of teaching as plunking information into student's heads.

There are a few other ways the three-box model steers us wrong. One is the idea that because there is a set number of things that fit in memory, as long as you stay under that limit in what you present to students at once, you're golden.

Like many other popular-but-counterproductive ideas about memory and learning, this one formed around a grain of truth. Closely linked to Atkinson and Shiffrin's research was another set of findings that came along during the early development of modern memory theory.

Seven Plus or Minus One, Chunking, and Recoding

In the course of developing all of these theories, memory researchers developed some agreed-upon procedures for measuring and quantifying short-term recall. Most of these involved different variations on saying back lists of numbers or words in order. Through these, they found that people showed a remarkable level of consistency in the number of items they could reliably recall. "Items," in this context, usually refers to individual words, or individual digits in a sequence of numbers. It can also mean other pieces of information that hang together, such as combinations of letters that mean something. Consider FBI, USA, LOL and so on—each of these meaningful acronyms would make up one item each, not three separate ones. The capacity limit of memory was originally set at around seven of these "chunks" of data, a number thought to represent fundamental limitations in our ability to process and make distinctions among incoming streams of information[18] that we're seeing or hearing. Later research using different approaches that helped control for the effects of strategy revised this number downward, to more like four chunks at a time.[19] However, that seven plus or minus one number stuck in the textbooks and in the public consciousness, aided by a classic 1956 article in which the theorist George Miller dubbed this limit the "magical number seven" due to its recurrence across all kinds of human cognitive capacities.[20]

The problem for teachers isn't in the question of exactly how many chunks (seven-ish, four-ish, or another number altogether) fit into immediate memory. Rather, it's in the application of the capacity concept to actual teaching practice.[21] It is a mistake to think that if you put seven bullet points on a slide, you've ensured that students will be able to remember them all. Each point may contain multiple concepts, each of which would constitute an item in and of itself. Unstructured or disjointed points, in particular, will likely end up being processed as individual chunks, quickly overwhelming memory.[22] Conversely, students might see conceptual relationships among your seven points that enable them to collapse the whole series into a single, memorable take-home point. Or they might fail to pay attention to your bullet points entirely, meaning that none will end up being remembered, magic number or no. (This point about attention is one we'll explore in a lot more detail in chapter 4.)

None of this means that George Miller was wrong about short-term memory. On the contrary, these caveats prove one of his most enduring points, one that is frequently overlooked when people reference that seminal article. This is the incredibly important role of *recoding*; in other words, the process of restructuring raw input into new forms as we enter it into memory. When we make up a memorable image to help us remember something new, we're recoding. When we notice that the letters F, B, and I represent a single concept that we understand, we're recoding. Even something simple like pausing for the hyphen between the parts of a phone number can be recoding, as we split up the seven individual numbers into the familiar three-digit and four-digit components. Recoding is something we do all the time, sometimes deliberately, but often automatically and unconsciously as we learn.

Whether we recode information, and how we recode it, can make or break our chances at remembering it. And so, Miller's recoding idea is an essential concept that has stood the test of time, both in practical and in theoretical importance. We may not call it "recoding" when we encourage students to organize information in particular ways as they're reviewing it, but it is. It's also recoding when students make up images or rhymes as mnemonics for particularly hard-to-remember facts. Even converting from one sensory modality to another—as when we visualize a scene we're reading in a novel, or verbally talk ourselves through a diagram we're looking at—is an example of recoding.

In sum, recoding information into chunks is something most researchers still agree is important for memory, and something that does hold relevance for teaching. Not so for rehearsal. Rehearsing items, in the sense of repeating them to oneself or otherwise refreshing them in conscious awareness, doesn't seem to have the power researchers once thought it did for converting information from temporary to long-term storage. As noted above in the example of emotional or meaningful experiences, plenty *can* end up in memory without us rehearsing it multiple times, or ever.[23] Further complicating things is the fact that what we might casually call "rehearsal" might not be rehearsal at all. Quizzing yourself with flashcards, passively rereading your textbook, or hearing something said to you over and over might all seem like rehearsal, but none of them, strictly speaking, are that. In practical terms, these activities would all produce very different payoffs for the time invested (an issue we'll revisit in depth in the next chapter). Like the 7 plus or minus idea, the notion of rehearsal as the royal road to memory can give students and teachers alike a false sense of security about what they're actually likely to retain.

Working Memory and the Idea of
Multiple Short-Term Memory Buffers

Since Atkinson and Shiffrin's seminal work, there have been some other major updates to researchers' basic conception of how information gets into our heads. The most important of these is the *working memory* concept, a school of thought most associated with the memory researcher Alan Baddeley.[24] Much of this theory has to do with elaborating on the component that was originally called short-term memory. Baddeley and colleagues made a set of compelling arguments, backed up with data from dozens of laboratory experiments, that this part of memory is actually made up of a number of distinct subsystems.

These subsystems share a common purpose: to hold a particular kind of information in a readily accessible way. For example, the "visuospatial sketchpad" keeps pictorial information in a kind of mind's eye. It kicks in when we are doing mental tasks where visualization is key: plotting a new route through town, predicting how our living room furniture might look in a new arrangement, working out problems in organic chemistry, or the all-important pursuit of winning at Tetris. Mathematical prowess, too, draws on this same ability to hang onto visual information as we work out a problem.[25]

Other parts of working memory are dedicated to hanging onto language-related information. A number of these components are short-term buffers that help us juggle the barrage of linguistic data that comes in as we speak, listen, or read. After our brains have decided that a given sound is speech, that input is shunted over to these language processing mechanisms for analysis. (Or, if we are reading, our brains convert the letters into language, usually by putting them into auditory speech sound format, and then they hand the data over to those same mechanisms.) Linguistic processing, especially speech comprehension, puts major demands on short-term memory, because it flies by so quickly and because there are so many parts to link together (sounds, words, phrases) in order to understand what's being said. No surprise then that we have multiple, highly specialized short-term storage systems for specific aspects of language. These include a system that holds speech sounds. It's possible that we even have specialized subsystems just for holding the abstract meaning of words, one that we use for comprehending language, and one that we use to store the meanings of words that we're planning to say in the near future.[26]

Each of these different subsystems works fairly independently, doing its own job without interfering with the others. Holding them together, symphony conductor style, is the "central executive." Besides coordinating among the players, the executive helps determine what is important to hang onto; many theorists today consider its operations to overlap a lot with what we would call attention.

Out of all these various subsystems, the one that's been most thoroughly picked apart by researchers is the one that holds a certain kind of auditory-verbal information, specifically the sounds that make up spoken words. Called "phonological working memory," or sometimes the "phonological loop," it creates the experience of the "mind's ear" that we almost seem to hear when we are doing something like consciously holding on to a sequence of numbers we just heard or read. It is this mind's ear that is involved in the kind of rehearsal that Atkinson and Shiffrin were talking about, especially for the kinds of materials used in classical laboratory studies of recall—lists of words, letters, or numbers.

The rather impressive amount of research on phonological working memory has turned up some key facts about how it works. It's best described as a high-fidelity, highly limited buffer; it preserves a lot of detail about the material within it but can only hold a small amount at a time. This amount isn't best measured in terms of words per se, but almost literally like a very short tape loop that holds a fixed duration of speech. This does vary across individuals; some of us have a larger loop that can hold more, and some fewer, resulting in a typical range that's basically the seven plus or minus two that George Miller hit upon so many years ago.

We also know from the research that *distinctiveness* plays a big role in how the phonological store does its job. Distinctiveness in memory refers to how much overlap there is among the different pieces of what is being stored in memory, in this case, how many repeated speech sounds there are—more repetition equals worse memory. With a short thought experiment, you can see (or, rather, hear) this for yourself. Try rehearsing a sequence of words with a lot of overlapping sounds, such as *awe, taught, chalk, shawl, hall, doll,* or *c, g, d, b, t, v, p.* If you're like most people, these short lists will overwhelm your phonological working memory to a greater degree than lists made up of dissimilar-sounding words, like *ask, view, rake, lamp, cheese.* Why is this? It's likely because your mind, in making temporary representations of those words in memory, is having to reuse the same components, and as those become difficult to distinguish it becomes difficult to maintain them all in memory.

It is impressive that researchers have nailed down so much about how this one piece of memory works. Careful, though, because just as with so many other classic findings, it's easy to misunderstand the role it plays in academic learning. Early on in the process of developing theories about verbal working

memory, researchers assumed, reasonably enough, that phonological working memory must be responsible for big chunks
of language comprehension. For example, this memory buffer
might be responsible for retaining all the different words that
make up a sentence until we get to the end and can figure out
what the whole sentence means. But as I mentioned before,
it turns out that we rarely do this in language processing,
instead zipping straight to the process of creating an abstract
representation without needing to remember individual words
at all. So while the phonological loop looks like a superstar
during laboratory-style tests involving lists, and is our best
friend on those rare occasions when we need to remember a
phone number, this component's involvement in academic
learning isn't immediately apparent.[27]

However, there is one single arena in which the phonological loop is absolutely critical: learning new words.[28] Whether
these are unfamiliar words in your native tongue or new
vocabulary items in a language you're trying to learn, these
new additions to your mental lexicon are almost guaranteed
to make a mandatory stop in phonological working memory.
In this way, the phonological loop's job is to replay and refresh the pieces of the word's sound, buying time while other
memory mechanisms create a permanent representation of
that new word.[29]

So unless you're teaching foreign language vocabulary, or
perhaps lots of new scientific terminology, this one heavily
scrutinized part of the mind really isn't germane to your
work. And while some principles governing it, such as the
importance of distinctiveness, are general ones, we should
be cautious about assuming that research primarily concentrating on verbal working memory tells us generalizable
things about how to promote memory in realistic teaching
and learning situations.

In sum, working memory theory is still considered current, and in my opinion it should be required background knowledge for anyone who teaches. In particular, it's important to take away the idea that memory isn't just one piece of the mind, but is many pieces, and that these parts all work in concert to help accomplish higher-level tasks (such as understanding spoken sentences, building vocabulary, or doing math problems).

It's also important to be clear about what researchers are really talking about when they relay their findings about working and short-term memory. When theorists use these terms, they are talking about the *immediate* short-term—the information that a person is actively thinking about in the here and now. Commonly short-term memory is talked about as synonymous with the recent past, as in, "my short-term memory is so bad, I can't remember what I had for breakfast today." Unless you're still in the process of pushing back from said breakfast table, this isn't really short-term memory as researchers would use the term. Once something goes out of your immediate conscious awareness, it's no longer the province of short-term memory, but rather, long-term.

The Three-Part Division of Long-Term Memory

What do we know about how long-term memory works? This is a question addressed by another classic framework for understanding memory, one that postulates three distinct types of memory, each supported by different systems within the brain. Most associated with the researcher Endel Tulving,[30] the idea is that long-term memory breaks down these distinct forms: *episodic*, *semantic*, and *procedural*.

Episodic memories are those which capture a first-person experience of some kind. When I think back to myself as a teenager watching Walter Mondale on television in 1984 badgering Gary Hart with the *"where's the beef?"* line—that's an episodic memory. When you walk into the university parking lot at the end of the day and flash back on where you left the car that morning, that's also episodic memory. Other highly context-dependent recollections are also episodic memory. Let's say that people in a laboratory experiment are given lists of words to remember, then at the end, there's a surprise test in which they're asked to identify which words they saw at any point during the session. The words would be long gone from working memory, but people might have formed a long-term memory of having encountered those words in that setting. If so, they could draw on episodic memory to answer the question. As a last example, when I'm struggling to recall where I left off in last week's lecture, I'm drawing on episodic memory. I haven't forgotten the lecture itself—just that particular class meeting where I was last presenting it.

Whether occurring naturally or as part of a contrived laboratory procedure, episodic memories are those that are tied up with a specific setting in a way that more abstract, factual memories are not. That emphasis on time and place is what creates the subjective first-person perspective that's the hallmark of episodic memory; these are memories that unmistakably happened *to you*, not to someone else, often including how you felt at the time, sensations that you were experiencing, or a physical location in the world.

When we are talking about abstract, factual memories, that is the semantic memory system at work.[31] Semantic memories make up our knowledge about the world, from the trivial (Clara Peller was the *"where's the beef?"* lady, the bolo tie is the official neckwear of the state of Arizona) to the profound (the knowledge base that makes up our disciplinary expertise, our understanding of subjects like history and geography, our vocabulary). This is obviously a vast amount of information, so in order to be able to navigate it in any useful way, our minds impose organizing schemes on all that we know. Especially in the case of people who know a lot about a particular topic, all these myriad pieces of information are sorted, arranged, and connected up to each other in meaningful ways.

In my book *Minds Online: Teaching Effectively with Technology*, I related an informal case study in which I asked a basketball fan to memorize a list of names composed of the top twenty players of all time. First, he was allowed to study the list of names, which I randomized before showing them to him. Then during the test phase, his task was to recall them in any order. Exactly how he did re-order the names was telling, as it revealed the scheme he used to organize the list items—first by the historical era in which each player was in his prime, then by the teams they played with and affiliations with other players (famous rivalries, close teammate relationships and so on). In this way, my basketball fan roughly replicated what has been observed in the scientific literature[32]—that semantic memory isn't an undifferentiated mass of information, but rather reflects the conceptual schemes people build when they acquire expertise in a particular area.

Linking related information together is one way we store semantic memory in an organized way, and that helps us when we face the daunting task of retrieving facts from this vast repository. If you think about it, it's rather miraculous that out of the thousands upon thousands of items in semantic memory, our cognitive systems select exactly the ones we need, effortlessly and almost instantaneously. We hardly notice the process, except when it fails. A classic example of

Chapter 2

this is the so-called *tip of the tongue* phenomenon, which you might have experienced when you tried to bring to mind the name Benedict Cumberbatch earlier in this chapter. Tip-of-the-tongue errors produce that unmistakable mental state where we know exactly what word (or name) that we want to pull from memory, but simply can't do it. The word isn't forgotten, exactly; if you're prompted in the right way, it'll pop right into mind. It's just momentarily irretrievable.[33]

One of the reasons why semantic and episodic memory can be so hit or miss is that they are largely driven by *cues*. Rather than, say, a filing system with everything sequenced in chronological or alphabetical order, long-term memory is driven by multiple linkages among related things. Some of these reflect conceptual relationships, like the teammate relationships that my basketball expert relied on for organizing the player list. Others have more to do with the context in which you first put the material into memory. Even when we aren't trying to do so, we take in information that's around us—how we feel, what we see, sounds, even the time of day—and this gets wrapped up in other things we're putting into memory.

We see this involuntary encoding of cues in the case of *flashbulb memories*, which are particularly rich episodic memories triggered by surprising, consequential events. The most obvious examples of these relate to big public events—things like the assassination of President John F. Kennedy (1963), the destruction of the space shuttle *Challenger* (1986), the death of Princess Diana (1997), or the attack on the Twin Towers on the morning of September 11, 2001. People commonly talk about these memories using some variation on the hallmark phrase *I remember exactly where I was and what I was doing when . . .* , reflecting the vivid and detailed set of cues encoded alongside the event itself.

It's important to note that these memories aren't perfect, indestructible records—despite the name's association to antique photography methods where a flashbulb permanently burned all the details of a scene onto film. Research volunteers questioned about Princess Diana's death sometimes remembered seeing a video of the car crash that took her life, even though no such video exists.[34] Those recalling 9/11 sometimes remembered that they saw video of the first plane striking the towers, although this wasn't broadcast until a day later.[35] Similarly, details like when the Pentagon was hit, or even one's own emotional reactions as they unfolded, fade and become corrupted over time.[36] As complete and intricately detailed as they may seem, flashbulb memories still follow the key principle that memories are never recordings of reality. But they do illustrate how our minds compile richly interconnected sets of cues during the encoding process.

Mundane memories, too, get bound to cues, enough to make a difference in performance. In the most famous demonstration of this principle, researchers set up a memory test with simple information—word lists—to be remembered under a set of circumstances that would provide a highly distinctive set of sensory cues. Volunteers, all trained scuba divers, learned the lists either underwater or on dry land, then tried to remember them either under the same or different conditions. Memory was better when the test conditions (underwater versus dry land) matched the study conditions, which researchers took as evidence of just how important those sensory cues are.[37] Provide the right set of conditions, and you remember; take them away, and you just might not.

Why would the mind set itself up to be so reliant on reinstating the context in which a memory was originally formed? The reasons probably have to do with making memory more efficient. When you consider just how vast your memory stores are, it's clear that locating the right thing at the right time is going to be a challenge, especially if you need to do so quickly. Using cues as triggers may help us cut through to the right information we need for a given situation, giving us a context sensitivity that lets us be selective, accurate and fast.

Semantic and episodic memory are often talked about together, because they have so many similarities: we tend to be consciously aware of them, they can be triggered through cues, they are organized along conceptual or contextual lines. It's worth noting though, that one can be formed without the other, even for the same experience. A good example of this is the phenomenon known as *source amnesia*, which isn't a dreaded disease but rather something that we all experience, sometimes embarrassingly, from time to time. Source amnesia happens when we remember a piece of factual information (bolo ties are the official neckwear of the state of Arizona) but not where we learned it (like me having no recollection of the actual first-person experience of having been told that fact). That source amnesia happens helps us know that there really is a distinction between these different forms of memory. It also explains one of the commonest memory failures that we have, one that gets even more common as we get older.[38] Teachers who emphasize evaluating sources as part of teaching critical thinking might notice this as well. It's something that adds to the already-difficult job[39] of developing critical faculties in our students—they may not even *remember* where they heard or saw something, let alone be able to evaluate whether that source was credible.

The last of the long-term memory systems that makes

up the classic tripartite theory is radically different from the first two. It's *procedural* memory, made up of stored information that lets us carry out processes and skills we've learned how to do. My ability to do a long-tail cast-on when I'm beginning a knitting project comes from my procedural memory. There, I've neatly stored away a program of sorts that, when I run it, tells my hands how to hold my yarn and the motions to make as I twist each stitch onto the knitting needle.[40] Now that I've acquired the skill, I can no longer easily verbalize each step of the process. This feeling of effortlessly executed nonverbal memory is what gives rise to the misnomer of "muscle memory," the phrase we commonly use to talk about procedures we know so well that they seem to have migrated from brain to body.

Of course these memories haven't somehow slipped the confines of the brain, but part of what makes procedural memories special is how they're handled within the brain. Unlike other long-term memories, which are distributed throughout regions of the cortex (the folded gray matter that forms the exterior visible part of the brain), procedural memories are housed within the cerebellum.[41] Similarly, it's possible to have brain damage that affects semantic and episodic memory, but leaves procedural memory alone. This leads to the surreal finding that individuals with this pattern of amnesia can learn a new skill (weaving on a miniature loom, for example, or tracing moving shapes on a computer monitor) but have no recollection of when or how they learned it.[42] All this together makes a strong case that procedural memory is a special form of long-term storage, separate from our conscious memory of experiences or our factual knowledge about the world.

Tulving's three-part concept of long-term memory has held up remarkably well over time. For anyone looking to use memory theory to improve student learning, the framework is a useful thing to have. It can steer us away from thinking of memory as one big undifferentiated bucket, while offering us definitions that let us be clear about what exactly we mean when we talk about memory in a given situation. The framework also puts needed emphasis on the active role of the person doing the remembering, stressing that we're constantly sorting and interpreting everything we might commit to long-term storage. This is all to the good as we strive to see our students as active participants in determining what they will remember, and in what form they will remember it.

Deep versus Shallow Processing

There's one last time-tested point from memory theory that all teachers should know about. This is the *levels of processing* idea, a concept honed by the researcher Fergus Craik and his colleagues through a series of ingenious studies focused on showing that what we do with information when we're first encountering it has a big impact on whether we actually remember that information.[43] There are a few twists on the procedures they came up with, but most of them have some variation on the following. People are asked to look at a series of seemingly random words, and asked to make a quick decision about each one. There are a couple of different kinds of decisions that can be made, and this difference is the key aspect of the experiment. In one condition, people are asked to judge superficial aspects of the word they are looking at, such as whether it happens to be printed in capital letters. In other conditions, they are asked more conceptual questions about each word, such as whether it could fit in a given sentence or whether it fits a particular category. At the end of the judgment task, researchers spring a surprise test on the subjects, asking them to go back and see which words they remember. Compare performance on the surprise test across conditions, and you'll probably see a powerful trend toward better recall for words that were judged on the basis of meaning.

Note that across the conditions, the answers are exactly the same (yes or no for each word) and the words themselves are exactly the same. The only thing that is not constant is the kind of question being asked, and by extension, the mental processes that are going on as a person answers the question. Presuming that people tend not to expend any more mental effort than they have to, they're likely to think more intensively about the words they are making conceptual judgments about, and to think less intensively about the words they are making cosmetic judgments about. This intensive thought, or "deep processing," helps drive the content into long-term memory.[44]

This one powerful idea explains a tremendous amount about remembering and forgetting in learning situations, spotlighting the plain fact that simply being in the presence of course material in no way assures that it will be remembered. It explains why students do seem to take away so much more when they are coaxed into thinking about material on a deeper level. This coaxing can take the form of the time-honored compare-and-contrast question, but it doesn't have to. In fact, one of the strongest permutations of deep processing has a distinctly more touchy-feely aura to it. Asking people to relate information to themselves—to say if they've experienced something similar, or even just to say if a term applies to them personally—induces the so-called *self-reference effect*, an instant boost to memorability.[45]

Good teachers frequently hit on the depth of processing

principle intuitively and through experience. Most of us who've been teaching for some time develop a sense of what kinds of thinking students are doing as they grapple with course material, and we devise ways to push this thinking deeper. Still, the depth of processing principle is one of the discoveries about memory that's most clearly applicable to teaching, and works dependably across all kinds of topics, subjects, and individual students, and so, it's well worth having a formal understanding of it.

The Flip Side of Memory: Forgetting and Why It Happens

For everything we remember, there's much, much more that we forget. Like remembering, forgetting isn't random; there are some principles that reliably determine what slips away and what doesn't. And as we see with the research base on memory, there are multiple distinct forms of forgetting.

The very first psychology textbook[46] I ever read had a vivid metaphor for the different kinds of forgetting. Picture a house cross-sectioned dollhouse-style. There are three different rooms, each with items representing stored information in memory. In one room, the items are dusty and rotting away, deteriorating purely because of disuse and the passage of time. In another, they're jumbled—intact but impossible to find because of the lack of organization.[47] A last room is bricked off, with access deliberately blocked for some reason—possibly because what's inside is too dangerous to deal with.

As metaphors go, this one isn't half bad. However, it should probably also include an empty room representing things we failed to store in the first place. There should also be another room where items have been added in layers over time, with more recent items obscuring and blocking ones the ones laid in before. This layered room corresponds with the principle of *distinctiveness*, which we also saw at work with the sound-alike words used in tests tapping the phonological loop. Similarity is the enemy of memorability, and when we encode new information, it essentially overwrites old information that is similar.[48]

You see this happening in the all-time classic forgetting problem of where you last left your car. You *remember* parking it, all right, but the problem is, you've parked it many times before, and those memories slide together to obscure the most recent episode of parking. It's the same thing when we rack our brains trying to remember whether we performed some routine but important task before leaving the house—such as turning off the iron. Or, when you commit a new batch of student names to memory, those start to take the place of last semester's students.

All of these forgetting metaphors hold up well in light of current memory theory, with one exception: the bricked-off room. Psychologists once put a lot of stock in the idea of "active" forgetting as a way to protect ourselves from trauma; think of the Alfred Hitchcock movie *Spellbound*, for example, whose plot hinges on amnesia caused by trauma. These days, psychologists tend to think that active forgetting is rare or perhaps nonexistent. Intentionally putting things out of mind is actually fairly difficult,[49] which you know if you've ever done something like set your clock five minutes ahead and tried to forget that you did that, in hopes of being early everywhere you go. There's also a suggestion, based on a contemporary study of memory among people who had experienced trauma, that we have better-than-average recall of *unpleasant* memories compared to pleasant ones.[50]

Deterioration of memory over time is another concept

that's been hotly debated by experts, who point out that it is hard to distinguish true time-based decay from interference stemming from other, newer items that have been added to memory (or in our house metaphor, the room where the recent items block the old ones). This academic controversy aside, it likely is the case that age and disuse do degrade what remains of a memory. As an example, in the first few years after college, large proportions of factual information that we acquire goes away and is gone forever.[51]

Other long-lasting memories might remain in some form, but decay warps them as their details are corrupted or confabulated over time. One famous study focused on a group of middle-aged men who had, as teenage boys, filled out a survey on some highly personal aspects of their lives: how they got along with their parents, whether they thought premarital sex was OK, and similar things that you would think would be highly memorable. When the research subjects were asked to replicate the answers they had given as teenagers, they were no more accurate than chance—as if a total stranger had filled the survey out purely by guessing.[52]

That's enough to shake one's confidence, but let's also not forget that what we encode in memory is but a minuscule fraction of all we experience. That bare room, the place where we neglected to actually put the things we might want later, represents this fact of life—that memory is a leaky container that catches only a tiny fraction of all that enters. For every crystal-clear Clara Peller moment we have, there are untold numbers of life's experiences that don't make the cut.

Memory as an Adaptation for Survival, and How Some of Its Bugs Are Actually Features

So are our memories really that bad? And if so, how have we as a species managed to make it this far? This question goes to the heart of what it means to have a good *human* memory. Let's remember that we're fundamentally unlike digital recording devices, whose value is measured in the sheer volume that they can hold. Our biologically based memories, by contrast, are judged by how well they do at helping the brain accomplish Job 1: Survival.

If we understand that one fact, it illuminates a whole new perspective on what memory is and what it is for. Instead of being a place to store things, memory is an ability that our minds and brains have evolved in order to keep us alive. Or in more nuanced terms, memory is a set of capacities that enable us to accomplish a range of important goals: communication, avoiding danger, prospecting for good things out there in the world, replicating strategies that have served us in the past, distinguishing friend from foe, solving problems and acquiring skills.

Seen in this light, the fact that memory retains so little begins to make sense. It is this selectivity, after all, that makes it more likely that we'll have only the most relevant, most useful material on hand, and that we will be able to actually pick out the thing we need when the chips are down. It also explains the exasperating, now-you-see-it, now-you-don't quirks of long-term memory. Having memory be heavily cue- and context-dependent might frustrate us when we're struggling to remember someone's name, or dredging up an obscure fact. The information is in there someplace, as becomes abundantly clear once we get the right cue (a place, a first sound of the name, even an emotion).

So instead of cursing our (or our students') colander-like minds and wishing they could hold more, we should feel good about the ways that memory does in fact serve us. There are ways to improve on it so that it picks up more of what we want it to, and we'll talk more about those hacks in the next chapter. But lest we wish we really were human video cameras, we should consider as a cautionary tale the rare cases of individuals who really do save almost everything. This rare and puzzling syndrome is called *hypermnesia*; the most famous example is the case of "S," reported by the neuroscientist A.R. Luria.[53]

"S" remembered a phenomenal amount of minutiae: the names of people he'd met years before, lengthy mathematical equations, entire conversations, verbatim.[54] While that last ability came in handy for S's job as a newspaper reporter, he was a far cry from the cognitive superhero you might expect. He had significant problems organizing and interpreting all he knew, and struggled to live a normal life. In Luria's view, these difficulties had to do with S's being unable to reason in an abstract way about the world. Poetry, metaphor, deriving meaning—these eluded him to an unusual degree.

It's not clear whether the problems that tend to go along with hypermnesia are the direct result of remembering so much, or whether both of these things stem from an underlying issue within the brain.[55] But many scientists have interpreted hypermnesia as proof of William James' words: "If we could recall everything, we would be as incapacitated as if we could not recall at all; a condition to remember is that we must forget."[56]

Short-Term Memory Meets Long-Term Memory: The Strange Case of Prospective Memory

In the time since the creation of the classic theoretical frameworks on working memory and the three parts of long-term memory, researchers have started to look at a completely different form called *prospective* memory. Even if we've never heard the term, this form of recall is instantly recognizable as the one we use when setting intentions. These intentions can extend over a few minutes (remember to turn the iron off before you leave the house) or much longer periods (remember to make a reservation for your anniversary dinner once a year). Prospective memory is also what we use when remembering *not* to do something that's part of our typical routine—like abstaining from food and water when we are scheduled to have surgery in the morning, or like stopping off to do an errand after work instead of following our usual route home.

Some prospective memories, such as anniversaries, appointments, or medication schedules, are triggered by time cues—when a certain time rolls around, we (ideally) remember to take the intended action. Others are triggered by environmental cues. Seeing your pills sitting on the counter, for example, can trigger the intention to take them.

Prospective memory is a bit of an oddball, fitting neatly into none of Tulving's semantic, episodic, or procedural categories. It's not even entirely a form of long-term memory, even though it's stored in a latent, long-lasting way. One of the things that makes prospective memory unreliable (and it *is* quite unreliable, as we'll get into later in this book) is the fact that some intentions have to stay active in working memory in order for us to execute them. Think of the "doorway effect"—the maddening experience of walking from one room to another in search of some object, such as scissors kept in a kitchen drawer. While you're walking, you stop thinking about the scissors as your thoughts wander to other things. Then by the time you make it to the kitchen, you've thoroughly forgotten why you walked there in the first place. You head back to your original room, enter the doorway and voila—you remember what you needed, triggered by cues in that original space.

This is another form that forgetting takes—an intention that we remember perfectly well, but neglected to act on at the right time or in the right context. Although it's easy to overlook, prospective memory is a vitally important cognitive process. This is especially true given our heavily scheduled, complex contemporary lifestyles. We can't always rely on routine or just follow along with what everyone else happens to be doing, unlike our long-ago ancestors. And while many of our slip-ups in prospective memory are trivial, others are not, as we'll see later on in chapter 4.

Why Do We Remember and Forget What We Do— And What Kinds of Improvement Are Possible?

No one can say why, on any single occasion, we remember any single thing. As to why I remembered Clara Peller during that one conversation with my husband, and not the many other things I might want to or need to in my life—that will remain a scientific mystery.

But all of the theories and all of the models that have been constructed so far can definitely predict overall patterns of remembering and forgetting. Emotions are huge, especially ones on the negative side of the spectrum; that's why a painful but powerful memory like being stung by a swarm of wasps will last a lifetime. Cues are critical too; even this many years later, I predict that if I were standing in the back yard of my old house in Alief, Texas where five-year-old me ran afoul of that nest, I'd remember even more. It's why the smell of pipe tobacco—the home remedy my mom used to make a soothing compress—still triggers a flood of sights, sounds, and feelings from that day.

Then there is the role of self-relevance and the connections between new information and what we already know. I remember that bolo ties are official state neckwear because I could hook those trivia facts to a rich database of other things I know about my home state, and probably also because that information is personally relevant to me as the spouse of an Arizona native who wears his own bolo collection on repeat. But in a classic case of source amnesia, I've forgotten where I picked up those facts in the first place. (Let's hope that whatever my source might have been, that it was a reliable one.)

Similar to being able to relate things to ourselves, the presence of an organized knowledge structure is another predictor of recall. Once I'd started to gain ground on learning the major discoveries, schools of thought, and landmark studies in the field of psycholinguistics, I began to be able to add to this knowledge base a lot more efficiently. Slotting new information into an existing framework helps it stick, and that structure creates additional cues and routes to recall that make it more likely we can retrieve the information later. Other kinds of organizing frameworks can also help; narrative structure, meaning the familiar building blocks and sequence we use when we tell stories, is one powerful example. Coupled with the element of surprise and a dose of emotions, narrative structure is what makes jokes (especially good ones) stick in mind so well.

By contrast, overlapping, nondistinctive memories tend

to fade: turning off the iron on any particular day, the details of last week's version of the Language and Cognition lecture I've given dozens of times, the names and faces of students in this semester versus the last semester and the one before that. When you couple these less-distinctive situations with a failure to pay attention, chances of remembering plummet. This is what happens with my typical parking job on any given morning; with me on autopilot and failing to encode what's special about that specific morning, the memory of one parking-episode slides into the next.

Other times forgetting happens through simple disuse, especially the kind where we don't ever actively pull the information out of long-term storage. Because the brain prioritizes storing what we need to know, it makes sense to decommission rarely accessed memories. In my case this meant the departure of the scientific name for wasps, which I once memorized but haven't needed to use for decades. Sadly, this also appears to have been the case for the history of Western civilization, at least the parts of it that I worked so hard to acquire my freshman year but never revisited after I dropped my final exam on the teacher's desk and sauntered out the door.

Knowing all of this, can we use these principles to set things up so that we, and our students, remember more, in a shorter amount of study time and with a good deal less angst? In a word: yes. The next chapter explains how—and why we should.

CHAPTER SUMMARY

- Experts agree on a core set of features and properties that make some information memorable. These include personal relevance, an emotional charge, connections to prior knowledge, structure, and organization.

- Conversely, we tend to forget information that is disjointed, lacks meaning, or is disconnected from our immediate goals and aims. Forgetting is also more likely for memories that overlap with other, similar memories.

- Contemporary theories of memory have largely moved beyond the idea that information passes through sensory, short-term, and long-term memory. The idea of working memory has been particularly influential, with the idea that we have several limited-capacity subsystems for holding information that we're actively working with.

- Contemporary theories do continue to portray memory as involving three distinct core processes: encoding, storage, and retrieval. Long-term memory is also frequently divided into three types: semantic, episodic, and procedural.

- Prospective memory is another form of memory involving the recall of intentions set in the past. It is typically fragile and error-prone, particularly in situations where a person is distracted.

TEACHING TAKE-AWAYS

- Students are likeliest to retain material when they care about, understand, and actively process that information.
- Although systems for holding verbal, auditory, and visual information are all distinct, our minds are good at recoding information across different formats and modalities. It may be helpful for students to deliberately recode material, for example, by visualizing a process they've read about or by organizing material from a lecture into an outline.
- Avoid thinking about memory as a container and teaching as information transmission. Instead, think about memory as a functional aspect of the mind, one that selectively and strategically takes in only the most personally relevant and meaningful material.
- Commonly, semantic memory is the type of long-term memory that teachers want students to build, as it includes facts, definitions, and concepts. However, occasionally other types, such as episodic and procedural memory, might be relevant, so it is good to articulate and reflect on exactly what we want students to remember so that we best know how to help.
- Because memory is so oriented toward retaining what we will personally need to know in the future, thinking about information in terms of the self is a powerful catalyst for memory. Have students ponder the meaning of anything you're asking them to memorize, and consider asking them how that knowledge applies to them personally.

- In academic learning, it is normal for students to retain relatively little, especially over the very long term. If we want factual information and skills to last for a long time, students need highly effective practice and deep processing in order to strengthen those memories.

ENHANCING MEMORY AND WHY IT MATTERS (EVEN THOUGH GOOGLE EXISTS)

—

If you'd like to get a roomful of teachers up in arms, suggest that their life's work is all about getting students to memorize facts.

If there was ever a school of thought in education that triggered backlash, it's this one: teaching that relies on repetitive memory drills, with the measure of success being how well students can parrot back information. It's an old school indeed, but the specter of the teacher-as-memorization-cop still fills us with indignation. Even those of us who are too young to have personally endured an actual rote-memorization drill still somehow have a sense of what such drills are like, and an associated sense of dread.

Taking shots at the idea of memory and memorization is a signature move of education pundits. The late, beloved advocate Sir Ken Robinson took this to a new level in his wildly popular TED talk[1] titled "Do Schools Kill Creativity?" Throughout the presentation, Robinson explicitly and implicitly pits rote learning against learning that involves creativity, self-expression, and original thinking. The argument goes like this: Traditional education has suffered with a fixation on what students can spit back in the form of memorized information, and in doing so, neglects and even actively obstructs students' ability to engage in sophisticated reasoning.

Some important context is that this kind of critique is framed, in the United States at least, against a decades-long trend toward frequent, onerous, and high-stakes standardized testing in K-12 education. This is a policy trend that citizens commonly despise for myriad reasons; in the minds of many, it's tied to the practice of memorization-oriented teaching. The complications around standardized testing in public K-12 education are beyond my expertise as a higher education faculty member, and one without a policy background at that. But I believe that tensions over this issue do bleed over into opinions about college-level teaching, leading people to reflexively dismiss the idea of building a knowledge base as any part of "real" learning.

We see this implicit assumption reflected in other ways as well. Consider Bloom's Taxonomy,[2] a scheme taught to generations of educators as a way to organize all the different things we are typically trying to accomplish with our teaching. If you teach, you've probably seen it in one form or another, usually presented as a collection of verbs: *know, understand, apply, evaluate* and so on, all corresponding to things we want students to be able to do.

Bloom's system is unapologetically hierarchical, which is why it's often illustrated with a pyramid.[3] And in this hierarchy of teaching and learning objectives, memory is squarely on the bottom. Whenever I look at Bloom's Taxonomy, I'm reminded of the U.S. government's food pyramid, where the bottom layer—remembering—corresponds to something like white flour, and the rest—synthesizing, evaluating, creating—lives up in the land of filet mignon, raw organic kale, and wild-caught Alaskan salmon.[4] The implication here is clear—excellent teachers don't spend their time in the bargain basement of learning, but concentrate instead on the good stuff up at the top.

That's the first objection to emphasizing memory in our teaching. Here's the other, more modern one: Now that we have so much information available on the Internet, and can access so much of it any time, any place, it's simply not necessary to commit things to our own individual memories. In this way, expecting students to be able to recall facts is about as up-to-date as the skills of the roving bards of ancient times, the fellows whose stock-in-trade was the ability to reel off memorized epic sagas to illiterate audiences in the time before books (and Netflix).

David Pogue sums up this idea in a piece titled "Smartphones Mean You Will No Longer Have to Memorize Facts," speculating that "maybe we'll soon conclude that memorizing facts is no longer part of the modern student's task. Maybe we should let the smartphone call up those facts as necessary—and let students focus on developing analytical skills (logic, interpretation, creative problem solving) and personal ones (motivation, self-control, tolerance)."[5] Pogue's prediction in the piece is that the memorization aspect of learning, once considered bedrock, will go the way of Morse code and elevator operating as an obsolete skill—and good riddance, because we instead want what modern life really demands, robust critical thinking skills.

No one wants to be the teacher who is obsessing over irrelevant, antiquated skills. Definitely no one wants to be the teacher who is crushing students' ability to think for themselves, their creativity, or their very spirit. So it's understandable that memorization is ingrained in our collective professional consciousness as something to avoid.

But there are good reasons to question our discomfort, and perhaps to come to some different conclusions about the value of memory and even rote memorization as part of what we do.

What's the Value of Memorized Knowledge in the Age of Search Engines?

Memory Supports Robust, Transferable Thinking Skills

The first such reason comes straight from recent cognitive science research on the relationship between acquiring knowledge in a discipline, and acquiring thinking skills in that discipline. As it turns out, when students acquire a more solid base of knowledge in an area, and when they do so using more efficient memory strategies, their thinking skills develop in specific, beneficial ways. The cognitive psychologist Sean Kang, director of Dartmouth's Cognition and Education Lab, has led a line of research that backs up this important relationship, demonstrating the ways in which strengthening memory using particular techniques leads to the ability to do things like engage in deductive reasoning about what you've learned.[6] We'll get more into those techniques later in the chapter, as well as looking at how technology can actually help put them into practice. Suffice it to say for now that there is a surprising amount of research already that shows that memory and thinking skills enjoy a complementary, not competitive relationship within learning.

This new science reveals another critically important

relationship. It turns out that memorizing information effectively, using active-learning techniques rather than weaker reread-and-review approaches, helps tackle one of the most stubborn problems in learning: transfer. Transfer is the process through which, for example, physics students understand that the principles they are learning apply across all kinds of different objects and processes—rockets, arrows, anvils, you name it. It's what allows a psychology student to see and understand common ways of setting up study designs across all kinds of different topics—things like control groups, experimental groups, and measurement scales. Transfer is what leads skilled students of literature to reach for a common set of analytical tools when approaching a work, whether that work was written a thousand years ago or last week. It's the process by which students make conceptual leaps between what they've learned in a single micro-context—one module, one case study, even one course—and new contexts where the concepts could be relevant. Transfer, in short, is what makes learning useful.[7]

Unfortunately, transfer is also about the most elusive thing we teachers ever try to achieve. This difficulty may reflect the mind's inherent bias toward efficiency above all else; by activating knowledge only in the time and context where it was originally acquired, we may save some cognitive effort and avoid traipsing down cognitive paths that aren't guaranteed to lead to success. But as it turns out, this design quirk of the mind is what makes it so hard to get students to see and exploit the connections between what they've learned and new material and contexts, especially when they're relatively new to an area. It typically takes students a lot of practice and a lot of insight to achieve transfer, and is an area where teachers typically overestimate how quickly and well students really are achieving it. And so, it's a big deal that reinforcing memory for basic facts in the field helps speed this process along.

Acquiring Knowledge Helps Students Learn How Memory Works

Deliberately designing a memory component into learning experiences has another side benefit. It pushes students to develop *metacognition*, which we can loosely define as knowledge about how your own thinking processes work, coupled with the ability and motivation to do everything you can to optimize those processes.[8] Metacognition has been a hot topic in higher education for a few years now, and it's not hard to see the appeal. It's a concrete way to get to one of our cherished goals, that of creating flexible, lifelong learners—people who aren't just holders of a crystallized body of knowledge but people who can easily add and expand knowledge over time, perhaps even leaping off into brand new fields. It's also turning out to be an effective way of leveling the playing field for students who come into higher education with lower levels of confidence about their ability to achieve in higher education, or a less advantaged background overall.[9]

So how does incorporating memory in one's teaching advance metacognition? One way is through encouraging practice of effective techniques. I think here about a traditional exercise that elementary schoolchildren do here in the United States: memorizing state capitols. In the age of Google, knowing capitols by heart is about the least necessary thing I can think of, except for this: It's a great way for kids to learn about the right and wrong ways to go about a memorization project. States and capitols are essentially a *paired-associates* task, in other words, an activity that requires you to remember an arbitrary link between two items.

As some kids discover on their own, and as other kids learn from whoever is coaching them along the way, paired associates respond particularly well to strategies like the *keyword method*. This method involves creating a memorable visual scene or story to trigger an association. When it's done correctly and for the right kind of situation, the keyword trick works amazingly well. In fact, back when I was a kid, I remember seeing ads on TV for a mail-order "super learning system" that appeared to be built mostly on this one single technique. To this day, I remember the cartoon of the letter R sawing a bunch of little rocks in half, which constituted the miracle, no-fail trick for remembering the capitol of Arkansas.[10]

Regardless of what strategy is used, several other truths are going to become evident as you work your way through memorizing all 50 capitols. One is that just skimming the list a few times isn't going to work—study has to be active, and it will work best if students tackle study in shorter spaced periods rather than in one intensive cram session. These are both bedrock principles of efficient study that we will delve into later in this chapter. Especially if students get explicit guidance in what strategies to try and why, and especially if they engage in conscious reflection about what worked and what didn't, an experience like this can leave them better equipped to tackle even more challenging self-teaching projects in the future.

Admittedly, this metacognition effect hasn't been explored by systematic research to the same extent that other connections have been, such as the connection between memory and transfer of learning. Nor should we conclude that it's a great idea to assign meaningless memorization projects to college students just so that they can learn memory strategies. But I think that when we do incorporate authentically useful knowledge, it presents an opportunity to help students figure out for themselves the best ways to make memory do their bidding.

Memorized Knowledge Is Useful Knowledge

Lastly, there are simply practical reasons to have some information down pat, even if it is something that's searchable. Consider what teaching expert James Lang has to say about the need for memory:

> [T]he Internet has made the storage and retrieval of information a much easier task for all of us, but that doesn't change the fact that we rely on memory all the time in the practice of our discipline and trades—not to mention in everyday life. An emergency-room doctor rushing a patient to surgery, a lawyer brought up short by a surprising piece of testimony in a trial, a sales clerk responding to an unexpected question by a customer—in all of those moments, the professional in question has to draw quickly from a memorized store of previous experiences and information. No doubt the ability to apply the information from memory to a new situation, and respond accordingly, represents a different and more complex thinking skill—but people can't get to that more complex skill without access to their medical, legal, or professional knowledge.[11]

It's simply not practical to drop everything and run a search during serious practice of a skill or profession, and thus, memorized knowledge still has value. In my book *Minds Online: Teaching Effectively with Technology*, I offered the example of what my colleague Liz Brauer, an engineering professor, had to say about her students' occasional protests that they didn't need to know basic principles of the discipline. They'd pushed back on her requirement that they memorize essential knowledge such as Ohm's law, saying that they could just look those facts and formulae up anytime. Her blunt take on this argument was that "if you have to look up Ohm's law every time you work on a circuit, you will not last as an electrical engineer." I think there must be equivalent sorts of knowledge in most disciplines—concepts that will surely form a stumbling block to fluent practice until you *don't* have to look them up.

Educational psychologist Daniel Willingham expands on the perils of the drop-everything-and-search mentality in a 2017 editorial titled "You Still Need Your Brain."[12] Using the example of beginning readers, he points out that having to look up multiple words doesn't just slow you down, it creates distractions that cause you to lose the thread of the text. Similarly, if you don't know the multiplication tables by heart, having to look up all the individual products as you work through a complex math problem will quickly lead to cognitive overload.

More subtly, but just as importantly, relying on our own knowledge allows us to better take context into account, compared to referencing isolated facts we're searching on the fly. This happens because the brain is so exquisitely attuned to relationships and conceptual organization in the way it stores and accesses information. Willingham offers the familiar example of budding writers who use words in totally inappropriate ways, reflecting their reliance on the dictionary definition rather than a deep understanding of the word's meaning. Such a budding writer might look up "meticulous," find that it can mean "being careful," and write that someone meticulously fell off a cliff. That sort of egregious error might be something most of us outgrow as our vocabularies expand. However, it highlights the critical need to connect information to real-world, complicated contexts in order for that knowledge to be useful. And that, in turn, is something that our brains do well but computers—including the ones we now carry around in our pockets—do quite poorly.

Getting back to the relationship between about thinking and memory, the linkage between the two should cue us to look at Bloom's taxonomy a little differently as well. The case for knowledge as a foundation for sophisticated learning is a strong one, but we should be cautious not to take the ladder, building, or pyramid metaphors too literally in learning. We should also be mindful of the fact that that researchers are still learning about the way in which the process of learning facts interacts with developing the ability to apply those facts.[13] Even if all the forms of learning represented by the taxonomy really are in some kind of hierarchical pyramid arrangement, that suggests the bottom layer is the *most* important of all, because it holds up everything above it.

In sum, the argument for including memory in our educational approaches includes both theoretical and practical pieces, all pointing to one important take-home for teachers: Thinking and memory aren't an either-or choice, and we do our students a disservice when we treat them like they are.

That said, we still have to acknowledge that there is a limited amount of time and energy available within any course, and thus, teachers have to be strategic about how much time they allot to the bottom layer of Bloom's taxonomy. Fortunately, though, there are ways to fast-track the process of knowledge building—not just with a few tips and tricks here and there, but powerful techniques backed by the kind of research discussed in the last chapter. These are neither onerous for teachers nor soul-crushing for students, and some can even be a little bit fun. The rest of this chapter is all about how to put these techniques into practice, especially with a boost from technology.

Factors that Accelerate and Enhance Memory

We'll start with the short list of broad, overarching factors that constitute some agreed-upon principles for what makes material memorable, especially in teaching and learning situations. Then, we'll consider some more specific practices and activities that accelerate memory. These practices also happen to be things that align well with the affordances of technology, so I'll point out some ways to leverage them using things like phone apps and the tools that are typically available within learning management systems. Lastly, we'll take on two special considerations in the question of improving memory with technology. These include the issue of whether knowing we will be able to find something online later affects our memory of it, and the impacts of technological aids specifically for improving prospective memory (i.e., memory for intentions and plans to be executed in the future).

As we saw in the previous chapter, the last few decades of memory research have seen the early, relatively simple conceptualizations of memory—the three-box modal model, working memory, and so on—shatter into a kaleidoscope of different specialized subsystems and more narrowly focused theories. Given this, it's remarkable that there is consensus on such a concise list of memory-boosting factors. Particularly when we are talking about real-world settings, such as academic or practical learning, psychologists largely agree on what kinds of processing strategies and what qualities of the information being learned matter the most for memory.

Here is what we tend to remember the best, no matter the situation or the subject:

Meaning and structure. This principle goes back to the idea that memory isn't a container, but rather, an adaptation that helps us accomplish our goals. Memory is most adaptive—that is, helpful to our survival—when it retains information selectively. Because we're bombarded with so much irrelevant and trivial information during every waking moment, memory needs to be fairly ruthless about what it selects. Just imagine if we saved every background conversation we heard as we went about our day, every random noise that entered our office during the workday, or every detail of the wallpaper pattern in our dentist's office. What a waste of space!

Besides being a great shortcut for helping filter the important from the trivial, meaningful interpretation also tells us how to store the information, offering points of connection to our existing knowledge. These organizational schemes are hugely important for allowing us to get the information back later. One organizational scheme that's particularly effective is *narrative structure*—that familiar format that we use to build up, explicate, and resolve a story. Researchers have observed that stories, even complicated ones, are especially memorable, probably for reasons that come back to interpretation and understanding.

Visualization. Human beings are visual creatures; natural selection has shaped us over eons to privilege our sense of sight over other senses, as our snouts shrank and hearing became less acute. The brain reflects this visual orientation, with relatively vast amounts of neural tissue and computing power devoted to processing the data that comes from our retinas.

It follows that among people with typical abilities to see,

visual information sticks in a way that other input does not. This isn't because they are "visual learners," a notion connected to the now-debunked theory of learning styles.[14] Nor is it something that's strictly a function of the way the input entered our brains in the first place. Internally visualizing information that came in through some other sense also produces a big bump in recall; this is one reason why the keyword method works as well as it does, even when learners make up all of their own images and experience them only in the mind's eye.

Other senses tend to heighten memory too, although not in the special way that vision seems to. When we hear something said in a particular way, or when there is a tactile sensation that goes along with an experience, those sensory details become yet another cue that can help lead us back to a stored memory. They also help make individual memories more distinctive, which as we learned in the previous chapter is particularly important when we have lots of similar memory records that overlap in some way.

Emotional charge. Emotions heighten memory, another principle that seems to link directly to the organization of the brain. Emotions and memories arise from structures throughout the brain, but notably, the ones that are most associated with emotions (the limbic system) and formation of new memories (the hippocampus) happen to be particularly interconnected. And like our other principles, this too makes sense from an evolutionary perspective. Emotions exist in order to help move us towards some things and away from others, so that we can survive and thrive in the world. And so we preferentially retain experiences that connect to those motivations.[15]

What particular emotions tend to heighten recall? There's some reason to think that negative emotions are particularly powerful.[16] If you're like most people, you know this all too well—everything from trauma to the various cringey things we say and do tend to stick with us, even when we wish we could forget them. But positive emotion helps too, and there's decent evidence that we learn better within an emotionally supportive and nonthreatening atmosphere. Lastly, the emotion of surprise seems to act as a potent memory accelerant. Plot twists in movies, unexpected conclusions we reach during a research project—all of these hit us harder emotionally and stick around longer than their unsurprising counterparts.

Attention. Like emotions, attention has an accelerating effect on memory. Unlike emotions, it seems to be necessary for most kinds of memory, especially when we are building a brand new memory. This is something that we'll get into in much more detail in the next chapter, which is all about the interconnections between attention and memory. However, it's important to note the importance of focused attention for practical reasons, especially given the folk belief that learning can happen without attention—that is, the learning by osmosis fallacy. Some degree of focus is needed if we're going to remember an experience later, and in general, the more intensely and exclusively we pay attention to something, the more we'll remember later.

Connection to goals. As we can see from all these factors, memory seems to operate on a strict need-to-know basis, saving what's likely to be useful and rejecting the rest. We don't tend to pick things up just because they might or might not be useful later on. Even willing our memories to absorb information because we think it might help us somehow in the future doesn't work without some contribution of all of the factors above, as any student can attest if they've ever studied for a high-stakes exam and done poorly anyway.

This bias toward the immediately relevant shows up in other ways as well. Reading instructions for a project stick with us when we're actually engaged in doing the project; we suddenly grasp the intricacies of tax rules when we're in the middle of preparing a return; we learn obscure medical facts when we're worriedly reading about a condition we think we might have.

Teaching Strategies that Capitalize on Memory Principles

These principles all have clear and broad implications for how we teach. "We do not teach brains on sticks," one teaching guide says, by way of explaining how critical it is to think of students' emotions if you want to maximize what they take away.[17] The same guide taps into the element of surprise too, advising teachers to provoke as much curiosity as they can from the get-go. Asking open-ended questions or assigning a short exercise that students are just barely able to attempt at their current skill level are both ways to do this. In one of the faculty workshops on learning sciences that I help facilitate, we do it by starting out each module with a short no-points quiz based on neuromyths. The questions essentially ask people to sort facts from common misconceptions about learning and the mind, and so when they get the answers a few moments later, most people are surprised—and also highly attentive, and ready to learn more.

Pre-quizzes or other methods for getting at prior knowledge also help instructors take advantage of the first principle: that we remember information best when it links up to what we already know. Traditionally, college courses start out in more or less standard fashion, picking up wherever students are assumed to be in their knowledge based on the prerequisites for the course. But as many teachers learn from hard experience, individual students can be all over the map in terms of what they already know when they come in. When instructors fail to get the lay of the land with respect to prior knowledge, we risk talking right past our students with information that is highly unlikely to stick around after they've heard it.

Similarly, the technique known as just-in-time teaching (JiTT) helps us adjust for what might be missing in students' knowledge bases.[18] JiTT works by having students do some kind of assignment, such as short "warm-ups" or mini versions of more complex problems they will do later, before a class meeting. Homework before class is pretty standard, but what makes the JiTT approach different is how the assignments are handled by instructors. They evaluate the work before the class period, then adjust the lesson to take into account what students did or did not do well on. Thus, instead of reteaching concepts that students already grasp just fine, the time is spent concentrating on the tougher material, which, if not addressed, can prevent students from adding the next round of concepts to memory.

JiTT also hooks into the principle that memory takes in material that relates to present, immediate goals (as opposed to abstract, far-off motivations such as an exam that's happening 2 months from now). JiTT is usually associated with classes that emphasize a lot of active problem solving, meaning that class is spent applying knowledge and not just watching presentations. By the time a student arrives in a JiTT class, he or she has already been primed for what the content is going to be about, and is put in a situation where the content needs to be used in the here and now. It's about as close to an ideal memory situation as you can get in an academic setting.

Speaking of problem-solving, another approach that capitalizes on memory is PBL, or problem-based learning.[19] This technique focuses, not surprisingly, on problem solving. However, PBL assignments aren't typical short homework-style problems, but rather complex scenarios and case studies that students work through, typically in groups, as an extended learning exercise. Like JiTT, PBL puts students in the position of taking in information that they're using in the here and now, not in the far-off future, thus accelerating memory.

Because it typically involves realistic scenarios and issues, PBL can also get students to care more about the material they are studying. In this way, PBL fits within the broader category of applied and real-world teaching techniques in general. Action research teams, for example, get students involved in actual community projects addressing actual real-world issues, not as a one-off "community service" activity but as a way to take material they're learning about and put it into practice.

These kinds of programs can have big educational impacts. A few years ago, one of my university responsibilities involved advising our school's action research program, which linked a set of first-year courses to a variety of applied, real-world projects. These included everything from building a community garden to leading discussions on immigration issues with groups of local residents, with students completing assignments along the way that connected the academic and applied sides of the course. These courses were a lot of work, but worth it, as it turned out. Our analyses revealed that these action research linked courses had multiple benefits, most notably, raising retention rates among female and underrepresented minority students. Students described this kind of hands-on work as challenging, but also engaging, emotionally rewarding, and relevant—in other words, a winning combination for creating lasting memories.

There are also the sensory aspects of the teaching materials and techniques we're using. Touching, hearing, seeing—all of these physical experiences add to the depth of what we remember and create distinctive traces that help make the memory stand out. One clear implication is the value of physical laboratory and field experiences, whose rich experiential qualities should lead to the creation of lasting memories. As long as the actions and sensations are reasonably relevant to the concepts at hand, they should amplify and complement learning. In other words, just having a lot of sensations pouring in during learning won't help, but if those sensations are meaningfully linked to the learning, they will help.

Because the visual superiority principle is so important, much research has also focused on the impacts of visual educational materials such as diagrams, animations, and infographics. This research has uncovered quite a few guiding principles, including the importance of conceptual relevance. Once you know about the importance of visualization for memory, it's tempting to start doing things like littering your slide decks with lots of random clip art. But based on the research to date, it's likely that decorative images don't enhance memory. Only those that convey content in some way—showing how a process unfolds, for example, or giving a pictorial representation of something described in text—boost recall of concepts later on.[20] Let's not forget as well that the power of visualization can be harnessed without having to set up illustrations at all. Teachers can ask students to create their own pictorial representations of what they are learning, either on paper, as photo essays, or even as purely mental images. These too will activate the cognitive mechanisms that make pictures memorable.

All of the teaching approaches I've suggested—pre-assessment, setting a positive emotional tone, just-in-time teaching, project-based and experiential learning, rich multimedia—are beneficial for all kinds of reasons that go well beyond memory. But what sets them apart is that they all jibe with the reasons why our minds retain what they do. And so, these approaches all have bigger and better impacts on knowledge acquisition than many of the tactics that we'd traditionally see in a university classroom. These traditional-but-suboptimal tactics include presenting long sequences of text-heavy content for reading and reviewing, with actual application just a speck in the far-off future.

Targeted Techniques for Improving Memory

The suggestions above are all fairly general guidelines that teachers can use to nudge memory along. Let's turn now to more narrowly focused methods that learners can engage in to build memory.

Now, if you ask most people about specific techniques for boosting memory, you'll likely get a description of a short-cut or two that they learned for memorizing information in school. These include the first-letter technique for remembering a set of ordered items (Every Good Boy Does Fine, Please Excuse My Dear Aunt Sally, and so on). Similarly, stories or even songs can be put to work as organizing schemes that help cue up information and make it easy to recall. In other words, when most people think of memory techniques, they're referencing *mnemonics*.

The keyword method I mentioned earlier, where an image is used to link a pair of items (R can saw—little rocks), falls into the category of narrowly focused mnemonics. So does the "memory palace" technique[21] that can be used to memorize complex sequences of information, such as a prewritten speech. Memory palaces work more or less the same way as the keyword method does, except that instead of using images to make associations between individual words, you make a set of associations between concepts and stops along a familiar set of locations. For example, you could associate each one of the main talking points in your speech with a location in your house, creating some kind of striking image to encapsulate each one.

Memory palaces work by leveraging our brain's built-in mechanisms for remembering spatial relationships and routes, coupled with the visual superiority and—in the case of weird or outrageous image pairings—element-of-surprise principles. When you follow the procedure scrupulously, it works like a charm. Once you've mastered the technique, and once you put in the effort to create and rehearse your sequence of associations, you can recall a phenomenal amount of information without using notes.

Mnemonics are great for this kind of one-off memorization task, and one I've used frequently myself to do things like give speeches without notes or memorize a set of names.[22] And who would ever manage to learn all the letters of the alphabet in order without the song—another mnemonic device that takes advantage of the way music is structured. However, mnemonics are not what I tend to emphasize as strategies for academic learning.[23] This is because they tend to be one-trick ponies, limited to only a very narrow kind of material or situation. To the extent that mnemonics encourage us to peek under the hood of memory to see what makes it work, they're a good thing. But there are far more versatile techniques that we can apply specifically to academic learning.

Here are the most powerful of these techniques:

Retrieval practice. This is far and away the star of memory improvement techniques; it manages to be both conceptually straightforward, backed by piles of empirical evidence, and usable across a wide range of situations and subjects. The term itself refers to retrieving information from memory, as we do most commonly (but not exclusively) when we answer test questions.[24] This idea might take a bit of getting used to in academic settings, where tests are usually cast as a way to measure learning rather than as part of the learning itself. But as we'll get into in a minute, there's plenty of proof that learning is exactly what happens when we practice pulling information out of memory.

In academic settings, retrieval practice can take the form of answering exam questions. It can also happen through low-stakes quizzes, which have become popular in education circles as a way to encourage frequent studying and provide accountability for doing the reading before class, while simultaneously reaping the benefits of retrieval. In my courses, I often make these repeatable for credit, so that students can keep taking each short quiz (with questions sampled randomly from a larger database) until they achieve a perfect score, if they want. Doing it this way defeats the purpose of measuring and evaluating student work in a competitive way, but that's not the point—rather it's intended to reinforce learning, through as many attempts as students need or want. And in a way, that's the mindset shift that has to happen in order for teachers to use this principle effectively, acknowledging that tests aren't just a measurement device, but a learning device as well.

There are examples of retrieval practice at work in all kinds of everyday situations too. Consider that little gate-keeper of contemporary commerce, the three-digit CVV code on the back of your credit cards. Do you pull out your card and read the numbers off every time you need to order something with it? If so, you're unlikely to ever commit that code to memory. You might have to go check it every single time, for as long as you have that card. But if instead you challenge yourself to try to type it in *without* checking first, pretty soon you won't have to. Even if there are a few bad attempts, trying helps, a lot. Similarly, if you want to remember a new acquaintance's name, the best thing you can do is try to use their name in conversation. But what if you get it wrong? You'll endure a moment of awkwardness, but when you hear it corrected, you're much more likely to remember it in the future if you just tried to do so on your own.

Retrieval practice has made some major waves in the pedagogy field, and rightly so. Rarely have we seen a set of findings with such clear and compelling implications for learning. I first started writing about incorporating retrieval practice into teaching in 2009,[25] and many others have weighed in as well, pointing out how this phenomenon can be leveraged to help students build a stronger base of knowledge, in less time.[26] The research on retrieval practice started decades ago, but amazingly, more findings keep coming out, even today.[27] Essentially, what the studies demonstrate is that when students answer questions about material, they remember it better and for longer, even if it's material they do not know well when they first try to answer the questions.

It's a remarkably robust effect, one that is hard to mess up no matter how you go about applying it. It works best when students get immediate feedback, and when the questions are open-ended or short answer in style.[28] But even the most basic of multiple-choice questions, even those with delayed feedback or no feedback at all, tend to produce some degree of improvement. This is particularly apparent when studying via quizzing is stacked up against other common approaches, such as rereading or reviewing material.[29] These common study activities may create an illusion of learning, as the material becomes more familiar, leading to a comfy sense of security that may not be warranted by the actual strength of one's learning.[30] Rereading may offer some other kinds of benefits, such as provoking reflection and encouraging students to explore a text in depth. But when it comes to memory, research reveals that rereading offers essentially nothing.[31] It's hard to believe, given that the preferred strategy for so many college students is to go at their textbooks, hour after hour, with an array of highlighting pens—but the return on time invested is vastly less than if they simply closed the books and tried quizzing themselves about what they just read.[32]

Furthermore, as I described earlier in the chapter, these memory benefits aren't independent from benefits having to do with higher thought processes. One way to pinpoint the development of these higher thinking abilities is to pick specific kinds of conceptual leaps that learners make in certain kinds of learning situations. Take the example of a person learning different families of birds. It starts with memorizing the individual species and the families to which they belong, but eventually, the learner should advance to being able to categorize new, never-before-seen examples into the correct families. This important mental process, called *inference*, develops more quickly when learners engage in retrieval practice.[33]

The benefits extend to physical or procedural skills as well. One study of people learning emergency resuscitation procedures, for example, found better scores on a final skills exam when learners also took tests of their skills earlier on in the course.[34] Even mathematical relationships that are hard to put into words are picked up more accurately when learners actively attempt to answer questions about the functions as they go.[35] And all of these skills and abilities are more likely to transfer to new situations when enhanced with retrieval practice, making it more likely that they'll serve learners well in the future.[36] In other words, when you solidify your knowledge using better study methodologies, it's easier to use that knowledge in a wider range of contexts where you might need it.

As if there weren't already enough reasons to take up retrieval practice as a learning strategy, there's even some suggestion that asking and answering questions helps smooth the pathway to remembering things you haven't even studied yet. Let's say that you're watching a lecture. Partway through, the speaker stops and asks you to answer a few questions about the material so far. The act of doing this actually enhances what you'll pick up later on down the line after the lecture resumes, a phenomenon called *test-potentiated learning*. This dynamic helps power the time-tested "SQ3R" and "PQ4R" strategies that students are commonly taught as strategies for making textbook reading sessions more productive. The "Q" in both refers to questions, and the methods take advantage of the fact that when you ask questions *before* encountering concepts, that primes you to pick up more from what you're about to read, regardless of whether you answer your original question. Even answering a test question *incorrectly* can promote learning amazingly enough, provided that getting the answer wrong triggers a student to go back and restudy what they missed.[37] Normally, restudying does next to nothing to boost memory, but retrieval practice creates an exception to this rule, creating a special receptive window during which restudied information actually does stick.

There are probably multiple reasons why retrieval practice works, which in turn helps explain why it works as well and as flexibly as it does. For one, it forces us to drop one of the biggest barriers to effective study, which is overconfidence in what we think we will remember.[38] Putting ourselves on the spot with a quiz exposes our weakest areas, which may not always be pleasant or comfortable, but that tells us exactly where we need to focus our additional studying. It is effortful and attention-demanding, which are both factors that enhance memory. Especially in the case of test-potentiated learning, retrieval may prod you to be more attentive during something like a lengthy lecture, providing a reminder to stay focused because you might be asked questions about what's to come.

Retrieval may even help cue our brains to the usefulness of what we're recalling, because after all, if we have to produce a piece of knowledge on one occasion, it's pretty likely that we'll have to do so again in the future. It is also just generally true that taking action tends to spark retention. Consider all the times that you've been driven someplace as a passive passenger. How confident are you that you'd be able to drive to that same place yourself? Now consider places you traveled to in the driver's seat. You're a lot better placed to navigate to those again. The active role matters a lot, even if you made mistakes or had to check your directions along the way.

Even with all of the great promise and substantial research associated with retrieval practice, the idea can be counter-intuitive or even repellent to some. Especially among teachers who are heavily invested in the philosophical stance that tests are a creativity-killing blight on education, having more of them is just about the last thing they'd want to do. In the

United States, we also have to remember that this is all playing out against the backlash generated by K-12 educational policies that revolve around lengthy, frequent, high-stakes standardized testing.[39] People hear "more tests," and they quite naturally picture the drills, stress, and constant time pressure that have indeed been a blight on America's public school classrooms for some time.

These bigger philosophical and political contexts are beyond our power to change, at least in the short term. There are some more specific objections to using tests for teaching, though, that can be easily addressed through the research literature we already have. Here are some of the most common themes you hear in criticism of learning that's stimulated by testing.

It doesn't last. This is part of the "cram and purge" concept that most of us have when we think of material learned solely because of a test. While it is true that information we don't need or use will tend to be forgotten, there's no reason to believe that material learned in connection with a test is subject to any kind of special treatment as far as remembering and forgetting are concerned. Researchers have also looked specifically at this issue, in order to verify that the boost they see from retrieval practice in laboratory-type studies does in fact last for any practically significant amount of time.

The results of these studies are encouraging. Attempting to replicate the kind of content and time frame that would be typical for a college course, one research study looked at retention for the content of a set of art history lectures. The lectures were initially spread over three days; research participants playing the part of students were instructed to study the material either through answering quiz questions, or reviewing written lecture summaries. Those assigned to quizzing did better on an exam held about a month later—a long time, as far as memory is concerned, and also very much in line with the time frames for retention that we'd expect in a typical college course.[40]

It's superficial, not "real" learning. Similar to the short-term learning idea, there is another common objection, that there's something fragile or fake about learning that's tied to testing. And we would want to be sure that the learning established this way does have the well-organized structure and rich interconnection to other knowledge that cognitive scientists think of when they consider the depth or quality of concepts in memory. This is also the kind of learning that does tend to be transferable, lending itself to new questions or new applications in a way that superficially memorized facts do not.

Memory researcher Jeffrey Karpicke takes on this idea in an article titled "Retrieval-Based Learning: Active Retrieval Promotes Meaningful Learning." He points out that retrieval practice's documented links to transfer and complex thought processes (e.g., drawing inferences) supports the idea that it is producing the development of rich, usable, high-quality memories, not isolated facts scattered here and there. He also notes that the benefits don't just hold for quiz questions that are repeated verbatim across study and test; improvements are seen even for questions that are quite different, or require sophisticated applications of what's been learned. And finally, it's hard to call retrieval practice's results superficial when they also apply to complex processes such as learning functions, and not just to things like memorized definitions or simple matching.[41]

Testing kills authentic enthusiasm for learning and heightens anxiety. This claim can be a bit harder to address, given that it can be subjective or even become a self-fulfilling prophecy.

Certainly, a teacher's attitudes about testing, coupled with the past history of any given student, could color how exams and quizzes make a person feel.

However, there's good reason not to automatically assume that retrieval practice's benefits come only at the price of emotional distress. One thought-provoking study of middle- and high-school students found that spreading frequent low-stakes assessments throughout a course—in this case, questions that students answered using "clicker" devices in class—actually *reduced* self-reported anxiety associated with higher-stakes exams.[42] According to the researchers, there were probably several ways that these everyday, no-big-deal clicker quizzes helped anxiety. First, they got students used to being in testing situations, building up a level of familiarity that helped reduce fear. Second, the clicker quizzes were simply a better way to study, leading students to feel justifiably more confident when heading into a big-ticket testing situation. These are all possibilities that do need to be researched more deeply. But this is a good initial suggestion that when it comes to students' feelings about tests and studying, quizzing does no harm and may do substantial good.

Spacing. This principle tends to be more intuitive, and an easier sell in some ways, compared to retrieval practice. Spacing, which sometimes goes by the name "distributed practice" in the scientific literature, has to do not with the way you study but in the way that you manage your study time.

Simply put, you get more out of the time when you split it up into shorter sessions: two ninety-minute sessions instead of a single three-hour session, for example. And, the more finely sliced and spaced-out the sessions, the better. The limits on spacing are mostly practical ones, guided mostly by how short a session can be and still allow you to settle in and focus, as well as the lead time you need to set up these multiple short sessions.

Telling students to follow a study plan, start early, and not cram have all long been standard study skills advice, but few such advice guides explain why the principle works and where its impacts come from. Like retrieval practice, spacing probably works because of several different mechanisms. One thing it does is break down the association between specific environmental cues and what's being learned, which in turn makes it easier to remember information when we're in a very different environment than where we first studied it. One side effect of a marathon cram session is that background cues—the place, time of day, even our mood and how we feel—will tend to get tied to the information that we are learning. We're probably more focused during shorter sessions as well.[43] There's even some suggestion that spaced learning helps stimulate the growth and survival of cells in areas of the brain that are critical for new learning and memory.[44]

That is the theory of why spacing works, and a large number of studies show that the theory plays out just as predicted across a robust variety of learning situations.[45] In one classic study, increasing the spacing of study sessions over time produced gains in retention that were evident *eight years* later.[46] Similar to the case of retrieval practice, it's not just simple associations or easy facts that stick better with spacing. Complex motor skills, nuanced definitions, difficult grammatical concepts, mathematical reasoning: All of these have been shown to benefit from this one relatively easy, straightforward memory strategy.[47]

Recently, researchers have also uncovered a new fact about spacing: It may enhance the effect of retrieval practice.[48]

Psychologists Regan Gurung and Kathleen Burns examined performance in Introduction to Psychology courses across nine different higher education institutions, focusing on what happens when the course design encourages more or less retrieval practice, and more or less spacing (e.g., through spreading out quiz deadlines versus having quizzes due all at once just a few times during the semester). Gurung and Burns found that these two course features interact, so that retrieval practice is most beneficial when also coupled with spacing.

High-Tech and Low-Tech Ways to Take Advantage of Retrieval Practice and Spacing

Retrieval practice and spacing are features that we teachers can—and probably should—build into our classes. Once again, that doesn't mean teaching to high-stakes, high-stress tests all of the time. It can take the form of "brain dump" exercises where students put down on paper everything they remember from a previous class or topic, as quickly as they can in any order. It can look like playing a Jeopardy!-style game before the big test. It can mean refocusing assignments around mastery, so that students get the chance to go back and restudy, retest, or otherwise reattempt work throughout the course.

Both principles also really take off when coupled with technology. Things like smartphone apps and learning-management systems go together with memory improvement strategies like peanut butter and jelly, which is a point I've argued for a while within ed-tech and learning circles.[49] However, this lovely synergy gets rolling only when the design of the tech is tightly aligned with the ways in which memory and learning work. Fortunately, there are some great examples out there of what this can look like in practice, and probably more in development as I type these words. The best ones to date, both in terms of overall usefulness and solid implementation of memory principles, tend to be grouped in a few major areas: quizzing applications, language learning programs, and adaptive learning systems.

Quizzing applications. One of the best developments in mobile ed-tech has been the proliferation of apps specifically for asking and answering questions. Whether styled like traditional test questions, survey items, flashcards, or competitive games, they're obviously in line with what we know about retrieval practice. When they're designed to use in short sessions, somewhat like the casual games we might use to kill a few minutes on our phones, they also take advantage of spacing.

My favorite among these is currently Kahoot!,[50] a program that lets teachers create fast-paced competitive quizzes with a variety of different question types (multiple-choice, true-false, and more). These can then be played quiz-game style in a group using any internet-enabled device. What I like about this approach is that first, students need not purchase or even download a freestanding app, but can instead participate just by going to Kahoot!'s web site and typing in a code that's issued once the teacher launches the quiz. I also like how it manages game play. Participants can quickly type in a name (I prefer pseudonyms over real names), and winners are declared after each question and after the whole quiz, based on a points system that takes into account speed as well as accuracy. Teachers can quickly scan a report after the quiz that flags the most-missed questions as well as the proportion of students who picked different question options. This is great for something like an exam review, where you'd want to hone in on the concepts that students are currently having the most trouble with. And lastly, the thing just works. So far, I've experienced mostly smooth and error-free performance from the system, which seems to be built on the philosophy of doing one thing and doing it well.

Kahoot! isn't everyone's cup of tea; in what the company describes as a deliberate design choice, there's a strict limit on the length of questions and answers. It also has peppy background music and a primary-color-heavy aesthetic that might not be adult or academic enough for some tastes. This is okay, though, because it is definitely not the only game in town if you want to ask questions for learning. Poll Everywhere is a well-established system that's mainly designed to stimulate audience participation during presentations; similar to Kahoot!, it lets you write questions that people then weigh in on using their own devices, but with less emphasis on competition and more on showing the distribution of answers. Quizlet is another one that has been around for a while; it has different options for mobile-friendly quizzes, with an emphasis on saving and sharing question sets. If you want to take a different approach altogether, you can use student response system (SRS) technology, which collects responses through specialized hardware resembling remote controls instead of through personal mobile devices. And by the time this book makes it to you, there may be even more newly invented options to choose from.

People tend to focus on the gamification aspects of quizzing systems, or similarly, on how the systems work as a motivational tool. This facet of the tech is important, especially when you're looking to reduce student anxiety or hoping to keep them engaged through tougher material, such as an exam review.[51] But it's not all about the fun factor, because something like Kahoot! can function as a near-perfect platform for retrieval practice.

Indeed, the research to date suggests that the effectiveness of such systems derives from their ability to tap into this memory principle. One controlled experiment revealed that introducing Kahoot! quizzes for exam review into an introductory psychology course significantly raised exam scores.[52] Other studies found similar positive effects for Kahoot!, but noted that these advantages weren't any greater than frequent, low-stakes quizzing done through other means, such as questions presented via SRS or quizzes taken privately on one's own device.[53] There's clearly a lot left to learn about the educational uses of quizzing systems, but for now, it looks like the gameplay aspects of Kahoot! aren't the most critical features that lead to learning. Teachers might choose it or another system depending on the particular look, feel, and pacing that they're after in any given learning situation. Ultimately, though, these systems are best seen as a means to an end—that desired end being active retrieval of the facts students need to know.

Programs for language learning. Here as well, there's one standout in the current marketplace: Duolingo. This system offers access to dozens of the worlds' languages, via a platform that is geared to short practice sessions. It is endowed with even more game-like features than Kahoot!, although these are less oriented toward head-to-head competition and more toward accruing points, earning badges, and leveling up. You alternate between pronunciation, writing, comprehension and vocabulary tasks, with a focus on practice, although there are also short stop-outs that do more explicit teaching

This is all a fresh take on traditional language instruction, and if you've ever tried it, you probably have found yourself carried along with its engaging little touches, like the jingle that goes with each correct answer, as well as by the rush of accomplishing each new level. Its fast-paced drills clearly leverage retrieval practice, with minimal passive exposure and maximal active recall. Spacing, too, is built into the design, both by breaking the learning into tiny micro-lessons you access on the go, and by features like built-in (and fairly aggressive) reminders to practice every day. This is a particularly good thing given that learning a new language as an adult is one of the most memory-intensive, cognitively demanding projects you can attempt.

One big caveat about Duolingo, though, is that it concentrates mostly on basic translation skills and vocabulary, not on the cultural and conversational aspects of language learning. As any professional language instructor will tell you, this social-cultural fluency is critical to actually being able to function in a foreign language. Thus, Duolingo and similar apps are perhaps best viewed as a way to build a foundation for becoming fluent, not as the road to fluency per se. But that head start isn't anything to sneeze at given the extraordinary demands of becoming fluent, and so, it's worth crediting Duolingo as adding something potentially quite valuable in this space.

So how does the research on Duolingo stack up? Surprisingly, there's relatively little research on it, considering its runaway popularity around the globe.[54] Studies of classes where Duolingo is coupled with traditional instruction suggests that students tend to like using the system, expressing that it does indeed have a fun factor that can be missing from other more traditional forms of study.[55] What about effectiveness? One study directly compared lessons teaching the same exact content (basic Italian vocabulary)

nificant trends across different
types of intelligent tutoring that
ything from brief laboratory-base
able to a single homework assignr
a full 8-week computer-based co
raditional in-person course. 46 of
ch studies that were incorporated in
show significantly better performan

rs have focused more on how students u
systems and on whether they like them.
ings are generally positive but not unive
daptive learning systems are not magica
harging learning, but they are one tool ir
lping students build knowledge in an effi-
dualized way, by leveraging the receptivity
g in something new when it builds on what
w.

nguage learning programs, adaptive learn-
ese are all technologies that can fast-track
e kind of knowledge we need to acquire in
the simplest definitions to some of the tough-
material out there (which foreign languages,
definitely are). We're likely to see even more of
s come into play as teachers look to use tech in
s in their own disciplines. I saw a great example
years ago in a faculty member's idea to use
ple texting capabilities that most students have
ones to leverage spacing and retrieval practice
te pharmacology program.[61] Students could opt
ltiple-choice questions sent to them at random
during the day, to reinforce material they were
n class. It was an effective, low-tech way to get

using either a slideshow-style, direct-instruction presentation or the gamified Duolingo approach. It turned out that students did like the Duolingo approach more and said that they'd be more likely to pursue further lessons with it compared to the more traditional alternative. They didn't learn more, though—researchers found that performance was about the same for both groups. We have to keep in mind that this study wasn't focused on typical use, where users decide when and how often to do the lessons, but instead scheduling use over a series of days. This made for a clean study design, but suggests that in realistic use, learning might be better for the system that users would be likely to actually use more frequently. That possibility, coupled with the emphasis on retrieval practice, offers some reason to believe that mobile apps for language learning can be powerful.

Duolingo may be the current rising star, but there have been a number of others on the tech-assisted language learning scene. Rosetta Stone and Babel are two well-known examples. They tend to offer more complex features (think live-coaching and sophisticated speech-recognition tech for honing one's accent), and bigger price tags to match, compared to Duolingo. But what the systems all tap into are the unique capabilities of technology to offer practice, and more practice, coupled with multimedia to support the many different facets of learning and using language. These features combine with personalization (e.g., rerunning concepts and materials that a given learner scores poorly on) and once again, lots of active retrieval. Taken together, it offers learners a real shot at learning a language more or less on their own, something we could have only fantasized about in the era before computers.

Adaptive learning systems. The personalization angle is front and center with our final category of technology for making the most of memory. Adaptive learning systems aren't as much the product of entrepreneurs cooking up apps, the way that programs like Duolingo came on the scene. Rather, they've emerged from within academic circles, where researchers in education and computer science have worked for decades to come up with programs that present concepts at the exact right time for a given learner.[56] They do this by attempting to detect the learner's current level of mastery of those concepts, and then using this information to target the information that learners are having the most trouble with while letting learners skip what they already know.

Besides this strategy of steering students through material in the most effective way possible, adaptive learning systems tend to emphasize scaffolding, meaning that they start with what a learner knows already and then add just enough, a bit at a time, to encourage the learner to keep stretching to extend that knowledge. In this way, the systems are solidly in line with another one of our bedrock memory principles: The mind takes in information best when it hooks in to something that's already there. Exploiting preexisting knowledge structures is something adaptive learning systems do by quizzing learners upfront, before presenting anything new; it's also why the programs sometimes offer hints rather than just telling learners that an answer is wrong before moving on. By calibrating the difficulty of questions, a system can encourage learners to tap into what they already know, and push them to persist in trying to answer harder and harder questions.

So what do these systems look like in practice? Examples of commercially developed adaptive learning systems include Cogbooks and Smart Sparrow, but there are many more.[57] Both essentially consist of the same kind of content you might see in a traditional textbook, presented digitally

and co
exercise
well the
might als
backgroun
determine
what mater
order. It's a
Amazon serv
instead of iter.

Another sys
Learning Initia
resource by scie
OLI pioneered th
at the core of ada
traditional textbc
content with this u
A distinguishing fe
on feedback, with th
tinually check and re
Lastly, there is an emp.
to instructors, echoing
and enabling instructo
trouble spots.

Surprisingly, there is.
the impacts of these kind
long they've been in existe
least one big meta-analytic
tutors"—a form of adaptive
improve student performanc
provement tends to vary a lot
tions.[59] Meta-analysis is essent
in which specialized statistical

conclusions about sig
sets. In this case, the
studied spanned eve
terventions, compar
or problem set, to
taken instead of a
50 individual resear
analysis did in fact
overall.

Other researche
adaptive learning
Here, too, the find
sally so. In sum,
means for turbc
the toolkit for he
cient and indivi
we have to takir
we already kno
Quiz apps, l
ing systems: T
memory for th
schools, from
est academic
in particular,
these option
creative way
of this a fe
just the sim
on their ph
in a gradu
to have m
intervals
learning

students studying throughout the day and throughout the week, and to do so via the most effective study technique ever discovered, namely, retrieval practice. For enterprising teachers and self-teachers, imagination is the only limit on what you can do.

Big-Picture Impacts of Technology on Memory

These uses of technology to fast-track memory really do call into question the idea that technology damages and diminishes human memory. Used correctly and in line with the research, it can do the exact opposite. There are some major strings attached, though. And I will admit that the research has mostly focused on situations where a person is trying to commit to memory some highly specific pieces of information—French verbs, classes of drugs, facts for an upcoming exam, and the like. These are not trivial. But it all raises the question of whether there are more global impacts on memory, reflecting perhaps the ways in which we use our technology to manage knowledge as we go through our days?

Research suggests that such impacts may exist, and in this case, the instincts of technology skeptics may just be correct. One of the central claims about how tech supposedly undermines us is the idea that we get lazy with memory when we think we can always just Google whatever we need. In one series of studies published in the top-flight journal *Science*, researchers attempted to pin down what exactly does happen when you think you can come back to something saved for you online, versus when you believe that you can't.[62]

In one piece of the study, research volunteers were presented with trivia facts that were new to them. They also took notes during this study phase, typing the facts into what they were led to believe were files on the computer they were using. The twist was that sometimes the volunteers were told that these files would be erased, meaning they wouldn't be able to look them up later. Other times, they were told that they would be able to reference the files, but would need to remember how to navigate back to the folders where the files were saved. The idea here was to simulate what goes on in our day-to-day technology usage, as we encounter information that we either think we'll be able to find again by searching, or not.

Everybody in the study then took a test over the trivia facts by writing down as many as they could remember. As it turned out, memory was indeed worse when people thought they would be able to look the information back up again. Just as the tech-skeptic view would predict, when we offload knowledge to the computer, we do seem to let ourselves off the hook for memorizing it ourselves. Conversely, when volunteers thought their notes files would be erased, performance improved. It wasn't all bad for the saved-information folks though. When they were told to organize their notes into specific folders, volunteers performed quite well at remembering where to find the various saved facts. In this way, researchers also reinforced the comeback from tech's defenders: *I might not remember everything, but I remember how to find it when I need it.*

The researchers also explored a more subtle aspect of the interrelationship between human memory and digital memory. They confronted a different set of volunteers with a challenging trivia quiz, asking true-false questions that participants frequently didn't know the answers to. When people are primed in this way to be thinking of knowledge and what they do and don't know, it turns out that they start thinking about computers and computer-related concepts.

This thought process might be unconscious, but is revealed through things like how quickly people process computer-related words.[63] Put another way, search engines and the idea of the Internet itself all float to the top of our minds when we're thinking about what we do and don't know.

These findings imply that search engines and saved files aren't just a tool we use, but rather, have become tied up with our whole concept of remembering and perhaps even knowledge itself. The authors frame their interpretation in context of a larger concept called "transactional memory." The idea is that even in the absence of any kind of technology, we don't draw strict boundaries around our own memories. Rather, we share the load with whoever is around us—friends, family, even our social group at large. In this way, depending on Google is nothing new, but rather, a natural extension of our human tendency to tap into whatever sources we can to extend what our memories can do.

> We are becoming symbiotic with our computer tools, growing into interconnected systems that remember less by knowing information than by knowing where the information can be found. This gives us the advantage of access to a vast range of information, although the disadvantages of being constantly "wired" are still being debated. It may be no more than nostalgia at this point, however, to wish we were less dependent on our gadgets. We have become dependent on them to the same degree we are dependent on all the knowledge we gain from our friends and co-workers—and lose if they are out of touch.[64]

These are some profound thoughts that both reinforce and challenge the idea that Google is undercutting us on a fundamental cognitive level. Yes, we do depend on it, the authors are saying, but the answer isn't to pretend that we can go back to a prewired era. Instead, the effects of technology are additive, providing a new, powerful avenue to do what we've always done—find and exploit the best ways to tap into the memory of everyone we know.

As teachers, we need to remember this idea of symbiosis as yet another reason not to fall back on the outmoded banking model of learning. It's natural, and probably advantageous, for students to find the information they need by any means necessary. But at the same time, we teachers should heed the risks of assuming that knowledge can always be reaccessed online. When it comes to the bedrock knowledge of a discipline or professional skill, students shouldn't fall back on looking things up. But they shouldn't just set all devices aside, because that would rob them of some of the best ways to put memory theory into practice. And that, in turn, is what being a discerning user of technology is all about—knowing what features of technology will help leverage the quirks of human memory, and which will not.

The story of how we offload memory onto technology, and what happens when we do, is rapidly changing as new research continues to emerge. There is currently some controversy, for example, over how reliable the "Google effect" on memory really is, with some laboratories failing to replicate the key finding that when people expect to be able to search for information later, they are less likely to remember it on their own.[65] Other researchers counter that some of the variability in findings can be explained by whether research participants actually trust that they will in fact be able to reaccess saved information through search—something that people would normally believe to be true in everyday life but might not believe in a contrived laboratory situation.[66] The current overall picture, though, is that relying on search engines for finding information does make a difference, one that may result in remembering less than we intend or expect to on our own.

It's important to keep the positive applications of tech for learning and memory in mind as well, especially where there have been some towering claims about how it affects our ability to learn.[67] But there's one area where technology's critics are probably right, one that has to do with the ways that technology can undercut us before we even get to the point of trying to commit something to memory. The next chapter focuses on attention, and what that means for focused, productive living when technology—and its attendant distractions—are usually right there within reach.

CHAPTER SUMMARY

- Memorization has been characterized by a number of education experts as outdated, harmful to student learning, and a diversion from acquiring higher-order thinking skills. Hierarchical schemes such as Bloom's Taxonomy reinforce the idea that building factual knowledge is a low priority in teaching.

- However, there are both practical and cognitive benefits to acquiring factual knowledge in a discipline. These include the ability to quickly and fluently apply what we've learned in a work or academic context, and the ability to extend and apply knowledge to new domains.

- Experts agree on several factors that makes material easier for students to remember. These include meaning, narrative structure, curiosity and surprise, visualization, emotions associated with the material, attention devoted to the material, and connection to the students' own goals.

- There are teaching strategies that align particularly well with factors that accelerate memory. Pre-quizzing on what students already know, just-in-time teaching, problem-based and applied learning projects, and well-designed multimedia all intersect with memory principles in powerful ways.

- Mnemonics offer limited use for most of what students need to remember in a typical course. However, there are more versatile techniques such as retrieval practice and spacing, both of which have strong track records of effectiveness and are well-grounded in memory research.

- There are some overarching, global effects that technology might be having on human memory. Availability of technology may lead to "offloading" information onto technology, especially when we believe we'll be able to look it up again online.

TEACHING TAKE-AWAYS

- Reflect on your own philosophy regarding the role of memory in teaching and learning. Question any resistance you might feel, asking where that resistance comes from and whether it might actually benefit students in your particular discipline to build a strong base of factual knowledge.

- Retrieval practice is a powerful strategy, but it also arouses concern among some teachers. Fortunately, it does not have to take the form of stressful, time-consuming exams, nor does it solely produce superficial learning that disappears after the test.

- Consider memory and alignment to memory principles when selecting technologies. Especially in the case of quizzing applications, language learning programs, and adaptive courseware systems, there are options that are both engaging to use and effective for strengthening knowledge.

- There are currently a rich set of outstanding technology options for running memory-boosting quizzes. Kahoot!, Poll Everywhere, and Quizlet are examples that you can experiment with.

- Be aware of the offloading phenomenon that takes place when we think we will be able to look material up online if we need it in the future. Consider discussing this phenomenon with students, along with the downsides of relying on searches for information they'll need to use frequently in their future classwork and careers.

—

CHAPTER 4

MEMORY REQUIRES ATTENTION

—

In the darkened lecture theater, all eyes (including mine) were on the legendary cognitive scientist George Sperling as he expounded on his latest project, a series of studies that built up a comprehensive mathematical model of the control of visual attention. It was the mid-1990s, and Sperling had turned his considerable intellectual firepower on the question of how we take attention from one location in space and redirect it to another location in space. He wasn't talking about how we moved our *eyes* from place to place, but rather, how we change the location that we're consciously focusing on. In order to get a grasp on this slippery theoretical concept, Sperling employed a physical metaphor: stage spotlights.[1]

As he explained to the audience of professors and grad students, what Sperling wanted to know was whether this spotlight worked like a sweeping mechanism, moving smoothly from point A to point B, or whether it worked more like separate, fixed pairs of lights that switched on to illuminate a new spot just as the previous one switched off.

Equation after equation filled the overhead projector as he walked us through the different ways he had modeled his theory to fit data from human volunteers completing meticulously designed research procedures. Then, as we sat trying to digest it all at the close of the talk, Sperling stood back, put down his marker and said, "Well, at the end of all this, I'm still not sure I understand attention. But I sure do understand spotlights."

Sperling was kidding, of course, and there was nothing frivolous at all about this work. Far from it; for years afterward, he and his research collaborators continued to turn out precise, quantitative theoretical investigations of how we move our attention around a scene. And as far as the sweeping-versus-switching question goes, his research came down solidly on the side of switching, where visual attention works like a stage hand turning fixed lights on and off in synchrony.[2]

But the reason why Sperling's statement has stuck with me all these years doesn't have to do with the intricacies of visual attention per se. Instead, I think it illustrates just how hard it is for even the most accomplished cognitive scientists to pin down this thing we call attention. Most textbooks at the time talked about attention in terms of physical metaphors, and many still do today. Popular metaphors for attention include likening it to gateway of fixed width that only a few things can fit through at a time, or similarly, a filter or screen that lets through only those items that have certain features or characteristics.

Additional metaphors include a camera lens, one capable of bringing just one thing at a time into sharp focus while blurring the surrounding background. Still others involve limited resources of various kinds—an engine's fuel, a computer's RAM, or money in a checking account. The popular psychology site verywellmind.com offers another mixed physical metaphor: "Think of attention as a highlighter. As you read through a section of text in a book, the highlighted section stands out, causing you to focus your interest on that area. Attention allows you to 'tune out' information, sensations and perceptions that are not relevant at the moment and instead focus your energy on the information that is important."[3] All of these metaphors highlight important characteristics of attention, but they bypass direct description of the mechanism itself.

In sum, everyone from the most brilliant researchers in psychology history to the most down-to-earth popularizers has trouble explaining exactly what attention is. Formal definitions drawn from psychology textbook glossaries aren't much better; they tend to be circular, never really explaining what happens in the mind to create the experience we all universally recognize as "paying attention."

How Attention Works

We may not know what attention is, but in one of the most delicious paradoxes that my field has to offer, we know a massive amount about how attention works. We also understand a remarkable amount from a neuroscience perspective. This goes well beyond the notion of just one or two "attention centers" in the brain; researchers at this point have been able to define multiple networks of structures and pathways that coordinate with one another. Some of these mechanisms are highly tied into vision, which makes sense given that we tend to look at things we're paying attention to, and vice versa. Others are more geared toward selective attention, which is what gives us the ability to focus on the most immediately relevant thoughts, sensations, and memories without spending precious cognitive resources on everything else.

So theorists do know the basics of how attention works, and they also have a good idea of what it is for—namely, to let the brain prioritize the most important tasks and inputs at any given moment. This might seem like a straightforward enough job. However, consider the fact that under this conception, attention really has two jobs to do, and these jobs are in some sense contradictory. On the one hand, there's the job of directing cognitive resources toward stimuli and processes that are relevant at the current moment—elevating or emphasizing those stimuli so that they take center stage. But on the other hand, attention also has the job of suppressing anything that's *not* relevant at a given moment. And so, these dual functions mean that your attentional systems have to constantly scan the environment for stimuli that might be important, select what's going to make it through to conscious awareness, and maintain focus on what's currently relevant, all while simultaneously deemphasizing or actively blocking everything else.

This means that even the most mundane everyday processing tasks involve a constant, finely calibrated give-and-take dynamic. Consider the so-called cocktail party effect, where you instantly notice your name even when it's mixed in with background noise. How is it possible to pick that one snippet of sound out of a stream of auditory input that you're actively ignoring? It happens because your attentional systems are continually monitoring the environment at a level below conscious awareness, processing stimuli at a basic level in order to sort out what's relevant from what isn't. Only after that sorting process can important information, such as your own name, emerge into your conscious awareness.

In short, human attentional systems have a wildly

complicated set of tasks to accomplish, and to accomplish those successfully requires discernment and a precise balance between letting too much in and keeping too much out. This is why my preferred metaphor for attention isn't actually a spotlight, gate, or highlighter. It's a bouncer—someone whose job it is to stand outside the entrance to conscious awareness, scanning for VIPs whom they want to usher inside, while keeping everyone else safely on the other side of that velvet rope. Doing the job well isn't just a matter of guarding the door—it's letting the right items through, without letting things get too crowded inside, and all while monitoring for potential trouble that could be brewing out on the periphery.

Achieving this delicate balance between what to let in and what to keep out, while scanning for possible threats, is what all of our brain's many attentional mechanisms are working together to do. And this process goes on moment after moment, throughout our whole waking lives. No wonder attention is so complicated to define and understand.

But in order to be better teachers, we do have to try to understand attention, because it is almost impossible to separate from memory.

How Attention Drives Memory and Learning

For decades now, cognitive psychologists have agreed that for all practical purposes, new learning requires focused attention. It follows that anything that diverts attention will produce a proportionate decrease in recall.[4]

The initial stage called *encoding*, when you're forming a new memory, is particularly subject to disruption. If you are distracted by trying to do something else at the same time or are monitoring more than one stream of input at a time, you'll encode less. One classic research project asked participants to learn word pairs while simultaneously monitoring another display. This kind of multitasking sharply reduced what participants were able to remember, especially when the distraction happened during the initial learning stage; multitasking during the recall stage, by contrast, produced smaller decrements.[5] Similarly, other researchers have found that in a cocktail-party situation, where you're deliberately screening out some kind of background chatter, you remember practically none of the content of what you screened out.[6] There's no backup tape, no way to rewind and retrieve something you weren't attending to—because once it's screened out, it's trashed by your cognitive systems and gone forever.

Technically, you *can* absorb information without consciously trying to do so, through a process that psychologists call "implicit learning" and what everyone else calls "learning by osmosis." This exception tends to apply most to the kind of learning where you are picking up patterns, rather than acquiring the kind of factual knowledge that we'd associate with academic learning. Implicit learning also surfaces the most when it's tested through means that are themselves indirect or unconscious. For example, you might be quicker to press a button saying that you recognize a photo that you saw but didn't pay much attention to. But if you're tested more directly—being asked to choose specifically which pictures you studied in a particular situation, for example—those implicit learning effects tend to evaporate. In sum, although experts might quibble about the extent of implicit learning under different circumstances, learning by osmosis is by far the exception, not the rule.

This principle effectively debunks the folk idea that we can pick up information without putting in the cognitive effort to pay attention to it—a notion that hopeful students might rely on as they while away a lecture as they are simultaneously engrossed in a text conversation, or as they attempt to study while consuming a steady stream of other, off-task media. Because distractions aren't necessarily just *external* inputs, but can also arise from our own internal cognitions, it also means that off-topic thoughts can diminish memory and learning.

Common Misconceptions about Attention

Given that memory depends on attention, and learning depends in many important ways on memory, it's clearly important for those of us who teach to have a decent grounding in core facts about attention. And yet, as I've noted, even scientists who study attention for a living struggle to articulate what we do know about it. Furthermore, there's the complication that attentional processes operate at least partially outside of our own conscious awareness, at the same time as they determine what we are consciously aware of in the first place. This means that our intuitions about attention tend to be way off base,[7] usually in ways that make us look more capable than we really are. The opacity of our own attention mechanisms then tends to combine with people's misgivings about technology to produce a few pretty big misconceptions, all of which can set our teaching on the wrong track. Here are the major ones to watch out for.

Scientists know a lot about what is happening to our attention spans. If it's meant literally, this claim is easy to dispense with. Here's why: As a cognitive psychologist I'm here to tell you that there's no such thing as "attention span."

I say this because the professional researchers working on attention almost never talk about it in terms of a time-based span. They may refer to its *capacity*, and perhaps even something akin to bandwidth—but they rarely mention set time periods where we're attentive and then cease to be so. Thus, attention span is more a folk conception than anything based in contemporary cognitive science. Our ability to remain attentive and engaged in a task varies tremendously not just from person to person, but situation to situation, and thus, treating attention like some kind of an egg timer in the brain is neither helpful nor useful. The span idea persists, though, and echoes of it crop up in sincerely well-intentioned teaching advice.

Students are attentive in class for ten minutes at a time. The most enduring example of this kind of misguided advice is the "ten-minute rule," roughly summarized as the idea that students can only pay attention for ten minutes at a time during a face-to-face class. It follows that instructors ought to switch up the rhythm of what they are doing every ten minutes or so, with the assumption being that bringing in a new topic or activity resets that ten-minute attention span clock. Or to take the idea further, instructors should perhaps forgo lectures altogether, given that students will only take in ten minutes, tops, out of any lecture they're at, no matter how compelling that lecture might be.

Incorporating lots of changes of pace and variety into a class period isn't necessarily bad advice, especially if the alternative is a classic extended and unbroken lecture mostly consisting of a lot of involved content. Incorporating frequent changes of pace probably does help students stay attentive, especially if the instructor makes a point of asking students to respond in some way by offering opinions, answering questions, or other active engagement in the topic at hand.[8]

However, it's a mistake to paint this practice as being grounded in an immutable rule of the brain.[9]

The ten-minute rule looks even more questionable when we trace back to the original research that it is based on. One red flag is that it is actually rather difficult to pin down those original studies, despite the fact that the rule itself is widely known and accepted among teachers even today. A number of the studies cited as support for it are quite old—think 1978 or earlier. Some are also way out of step with contemporary research standards, for example, using data gathered via casual observation by observers who are sometimes present in class, and sometimes not.[10] Furthermore, many use measures whose relationship to actual attentiveness are tenuous at best. Some, for example, rely on the volume of student note-taking as a proxy for attentiveness, despite multiple alternative explanations for why students might write more or less throughout a given class period. With all this in mind, we can confidently set the ten-minute rule aside as an idea borne more out of intuition than rigorous, up-to-date science.

Technology is to blame for shrinking attentional capacity. Even if we don't take literally the idea that attention works on a set time basis, and if we take the ten-minute rule with a liberal amount of salt, isn't it still the case that our overall ability to pay attention is decreasing in contemporary times? This claim is another idea that's repeated so much that it's commonly taken as fact, especially when it's linked to the unrelenting inroads of technology into our lives. But even more so than we saw with the ten-minute rule, the research basis for this claim is gossamer-thin.

Take one research finding that was shared all over the globe, a study purporting to show that that human attention spans had shrunk to below that of the average *goldfish,* presumably because we all now spend so much time online. Setting aside the fact that attention span is not a thing, why should we be skeptical of this claim? First of all, don't assume that just because this study was cited all over the world, it must have come from a high-profile peer-reviewed journal. It was actually just an internal project commissioned by the software company Microsoft and pushed out with no real scientific vetting at all.[11] As for the goldfish "control group," what the researchers were actually looking at among these little creatures was working memory, not attention. It's certainly an interesting line of neuropsychological research on nonhuman animals, but not one that provides any kind of meaningful comparison to students focusing (or not) on schoolwork.[12]

Even if the human-versus-goldfish study *had* been an actual peer-reviewed project, it still wouldn't have offered good information on attention span, because the measure they focused on among the human participants was subjective impressions of one's own attention span. This is problematic for multiple reasons. For one, there's no reason to think that anyone could accurately pinpoint this for themselves, given the limited insight we have into our own attentional processes and the fact that many of them operate out of conscious awareness. Asking people directly if they think their attention spans have declined is also a picture-perfect example of what researchers call "demand characteristics," whereby experimenters subtly telegraph the expected responses to participants, setting up a self-fulfilling prophecy.

Clearly, then, we can dispense with the goldfish study as a reason to think that technology has caused wholesale decline in the ability to pay sustained attention. That's not to say that engaging in particular cognitive activities linked to tech couldn't cause that kind of global change, because in theory it could. One intriguing line of cross-cultural research, for example, contrasted cognitive characteristics of kids growing up in rural Maya Mexico versus the urban United States.[13] In both cases, the children were engaged with technology, but of vastly different sorts. In the United States, it was with video games of various kinds, but in Mexico, it was with traditional backstrap loom weaving. The authors concluded that observing loom weaving for hours at a time—as children commonly did, as a way to learn—led to the rural Mexican children's being able to comfortably focus for longer periods of time than their urban U.S. counterparts.

It's a stretch to conclude from this line of research that constant technology use automatically degrades attention, but it sheds some light on the possibility of some level of change by directly connecting the nature of the technology engagement (long periods of watching versus frequent fast-paced switching among stimuli) with the way that attention might be changed. Still, it's not enough to completely support the claim that people these days just can't handle life without a constant stream of high stimulation.

However, an eroding ability to focus is something that many people swear up and down that they subjectively feel. Is there a ready explanation for this disconnect between perception and scientific reality? Not at the moment, but I look at it this way: Our ability to stay attentive even when we're bored or disengaged may not have decreased, but perhaps our *willingness* has. In other words, we may have experienced a global decrease in our tolerance for the discomfort of empty time or activities that aren't that enticing. Perhaps it fits with the many other ways in which affluent modern people chafe at discomforts that our ancestors tolerated with minimal complaint. There was the heat, the cold, even constant bouts with hunger and thirst—not pleasant, to be sure, but something that people were used to because it was simply a part of life. Maybe today, boredom is a little bit like those states.

In sum: Do people need breaks from sustained mental effort? Yes. Is it a good idea for teachers to alternate lecturing with other activities? Yes. Does technology alter our preferences and typical patterns associated with paying attention? Possibly. But none of these conclusions have all that much to do with attention span.

Consuming a steady stream of content from our digital devices burns us out mentally and neurologically. One of the most-discussed complaints regarding technology and attention is the tired, edgy, unsatisfied mental state we find ourselves in after a bout of scrolling, tab-switching, and headline scanning. Especially if we've engaged in this kind of tech-skimming as an (ineffective) way to take a break from work that also happened to take place online, it can feel like the screen itself is what has drained our mental energy.

But tempting as it may be to conclude that a techno-binge has fried our brains right down to our very neurons, it's worth noting that this is another concept stemming from pop culture and marketing, not neuroscience. It's related to the idea of "continuous partial attention," a term invented by the software and technology consultant Linda Stone.[14] The phrase refers to the habit of spreading attention across multiple inputs without focusing intently on any single one, as we might do if we're trying to work on a project while responding to incoming email notifications, toggling over to Twitter, and fielding the occasional Slack[15] message.

We engage in continuous partial attention because we're afraid of missing out on anything that might potentially be important, even though it's ultimately self-defeating. According to Stone, it causes a host of ills ranging from feeling overwhelmed and powerless to decreasing creativity. Similarly, Gary Small, who led the "Your Brain on Google" project discussed in chapter 1, talks about "techno-brain burnout" as a description of what happens when we spend too much time on devices.

As subjective descriptions of how tech binges make us feel, these ideas are spot-on. But we have to keep in mind they are just that: subjective descriptions. There's little evidence to suggest that they correspond to any kind of tangible process going on in the brain's attention mechanisms. Nor are they necessarily any more pernicious than, say, the dissatisfaction we might feel after aimlessly channel-surfing on television or skimming through a trashy magazine. That bad feeling we might have in the moment does not necessarily mean that we've somehow tweaked the inner workings of the brain.

That said, it's worth acknowledging that burnout in the traditional sense probably *is* accelerated by technology. Chronic overwork, coupled with the onset of work-related cynicism and never feeling like your efforts are adequate to meet demand, does indeed create a toxic brew when phones and messaging apps are there to create the illusion of being on duty 24–7.[16] There are also very real concerns about technology's effects on sleep. It may not have the same novelty value as a cool new brain syndrome, but sleep deprivation really does torpedo the brain's ability to function.

Teenagers in particular are susceptible to ending up chronically overtired when they take phones to bed,[17] as they are incredibly tempted to do by a culture of intense, always-on social media presence and the primacy of text messaging as a way of socializing with peers. One study found that among teens who are particularly plagued with FOMO (fear of missing out), sleep can be disturbed even when the phone is off and out of reach.[18] This happens because, amazingly enough, anxiety about social disconnection stalks these teenagers even when they are offline, producing bouts of late-night wakefulness.

So for all of these old-school, unglamorous reasons—improving sleep, setting appropriate work boundaries, resisting FOMO—having a conscious plan to moderate how we use our devices is a great idea. However, just as the ten-minute rule is good advice grounded in bad reasoning, the caution against techno-brain burnout is good advice wrapped up in an unnecessary layer of pseudoscience. If you feel that technology is making you unhappy, tired, and stressed, well, it probably is. There's also not much of a downside to scrutinizing how and how frequently you use your personal technology. But don't worry—your neurons aren't paying a price if you choose to spend a lot of time in front of a screen.

The brain can't multitask. This is one that I've frequently heard and read over the last several years.[19] Generally it comes wrapped in caution about the illusion of productivity created by juggling several tasks at once, much like with the continuous partial attention concept. And, it is grounded to an extent in the research literature on attention, particularly research having to do with task switching, which we will get to in a moment. But it's important to note that this statement isn't literally true. Accepting it as such leads us to an overly rigid conception of what happens during divided attention, and muddies the issue of how multitasking gets in the way of memory and learning.

When we look at the big picture of how our neural systems work, it's clear that not only *can* the brain multitask, it lives to multitask. Fundamentally, the brain is organized as a massive parallel processing system, with multiple different systems all working side by side to accomplish different jobs: processing sensory input, running the body's life support systems, creating emotions, decoding language, and on and on.

Cognitive systems, too, are organized and coordinated in a way that allows different distinct mechanisms to handle different tasks at the same time. Our systems for processing language are a particularly good example of this. At any given moment, various subsystems are independently forming and maintaining memories for the way words sound, what they mean, and even our plans for what we want to say next. All of this work gets seamlessly integrated at the point where we're speaking and understanding, but before then, the brain is feverishly divvying up and delegating distinct tasks for distinct systems to manage, all at the same time.

When multitasking is framed in terms of cognitive processes that operate in parallel, it reveals other exceptions to the multitasking rule. Cognitive processes actually run pretty well in parallel as long as they (a) don't require much in the form of decision-making or other "executive" functions, and (b) tap into separate cognitive mechanisms. Think about listening to a podcast while driving, watching a movie while knitting, or reading a book while riding a stationary bike (which you might in fact be doing right now). Yes, if the cognitive demands on either task suddenly spike—you encounter a road hazard, the mind-bending plot twist is revealed, you lose your place in the book and have to find it again—you'll probably put one of the tasks on pause. But as cognitive psychologists have observed time and again,[20] some processes run fairly well concurrently, while others clash with each other. It really has to do with the degree of separation between the parts of the mind that are doing most of the work.

However, even though literal claims about the multitasking brain may not be true, we should give credit to the anti-multitasking critics for picking up on something that *is* true about certain kinds of processing. As I talked about earlier in this chapter, demanding cognitive tasks like acquiring new learning do require focused attention. The bandwidth we have for doing this truly is quite limited, perhaps to as little as one thing at a time. It's absolutely the case that we can't effectively multitask as far as conscious, intensive processing of the sort that's most relevant to academic learning.

What the critics may also be tapping into is research not on brain multitasking per se, but rather, on task switching. A number of studies[21] have focused on what are called "switch costs," meaning the time cost (and sometimes, loss of accuracy) that happens when we shift focus from one task to another. The switch cost concept is particularly relevant to what happens during real-world technology use. Think of a person who's responding to email messages, checking social media, and answering phone calls from home at the same time as they are plowing through a demanding work project. This typical modern employee is paying a price for each one of these diversions, which makes the main project take more time overall (and probably decreases the quality of the work they are doing on each of those side tasks as well).[22]

Estimates vary as to exactly how many seconds or minutes it takes to get back into the swing of one activity once we've switched to another activity. But even if we can't pinpoint the exact amount, it's safe to say that task switching probably does drain off time. It also falls right in line with the claim that when we think we're capably doing lots of things at once, we're probably just toggling, and inefficiently at that.

Overall, technology probably doesn't have long-term, global impacts on attention through shortening span or triggering brain burnout. And multitasking is something our brains do handily, just not when we are talking about the kind of focused processing that is needed for more demanding cognitive tasks. But the core affordances of technology—immediacy, the ability to generate almost infinite numbers of reminders, notifications, and pings, engaging us with seemingly endless relevant content—do have impacts, at least in the short term. We'll get into those specifically associated with portable technology in the next chapter. But in general, we should have a cautious optimism about our own ability to pay attention—and therefore, to remember—in a distracting world.

Technology, Attention, and Prospective Memory

Attention is particularly critical for prospective memory, the form of memory that allows us to follow through on intentions at the right time and place. Examples include remembering to bring a reusable bag into the supermarket, to switch off the kitchen lights before we go to bed, or to take the just-purchased groceries off the roof of the car before driving away. This form of memory has some unique characteristics compared to other forms (e.g., semantic or episodic memory). Thus, we can expect that it will interact in different ways with technology, compared to other forms. Some of these impacts are positive, such that technology will be helpful in bolstering prospective memory, but others are clearly negative, as we'll get into in the section below.

First, though, what are these unique characteristics? Prospective memory is a kind of hybrid between our long-term memory, working memory, and attention. In order to hang onto an intention long enough to execute it, it has to be kept fresh in awareness, which draws heavily on attention. Anything that takes focus off of an intention increases the risk of forgetting to follow through on the intention. This could be something else we're doing at the same time, an interruption, a switch to a new activity. Once the intention has left awareness, it can still be revived by a cue in the environment—some trigger or sensation that leads one back to the original intent—given that the intention is still stored in long-term memory. But, when both these angles—cues and maintaining awareness—fall through, the chances of failure skyrocket.

It really does not take much to induce this kind of memory failure. One of my graduate students, Oz Rico, invented a procedure to cause our traditional college-aged research volunteers to forget instructions in a simple computer task, one that asked them to identify photos of celebrities and say whether the celebrities were wearing glasses in the photos. In between giving the instructions and launching the task, Oz diverted our volunteers' attention by handing them an intentionally nonfunctioning pen to fill out some required preexperiment paperwork and then leaving the room. After spending a little while ineffectively scratching around with the sabotaged writing instrument, the volunteers had to go down the hall to track down Oz and ask for a new one. He engaged them in a little bit of small talk and sent them back, where a significant number of them then forgot to follow through on the trivial task they were supposed to be doing. Other laboratory procedures for inducing prospective memory failures have people do things like monitor word lists for particular target letters ("press the space bar any time you see the letter D") while doing other tasks. Generally, such procedures show that under these kinds of challenging conditions, intentions can be forgotten in mere minutes.

You can also see this phenomenon in the annoying case of the *doorway effect*, where we walk into different rooms and forget why we're there, only to immediately remember when we give up and go back to wherever we were before. When we head out on our little journey off to the kitchen for, say, the scissors, we're paying attention to the reason we need the scissors, but that attentiveness doesn't last long. Frequently, attention is diverted by all the things we see and think about along the way. Thus, when we arrive at our destination, there's nothing around us to cue up the original intention; instead, we're surrounded by misleading or irrelevant cues, things that don't have anything to do with the task we were engaged in.

In a sense, the trip around the house is an interruption to our attention and the natural flow of the task, and this interruption is key to setting us up for failure. Unfortunately, in many real-life situations, the consequences of this kind of failure can be a lot worse than having to make an extra trip down the hall. Prospective memory lapses have been blamed for an array of catastrophic mistakes, including a 1987 plane crash attributed to a momentary distraction that caused the crew to forget to set the flaps before takeoff.[23] Distractions are also the culprit for medical mishaps ranging from nurses' neglecting to dispense the right medication to surgical teams' leaving instruments inside their patients before closing up.[24] Saddest of all are the multiple cases of tired, preoccupied parents who forget to remove children from the back seat when they exit their cars.[25]

Besides emphasizing how important prospective memory is in the real world, these tragic examples bring to the forefront another unsettling fact about memory: Just wanting to remember an intention isn't enough to ensure that you do. In this way, our priorities and even our emotions take a back seat to circumstances. Because prospective memory is so heavily driven by where we're focusing at any given moment, and by cues in the environment, those factors tend to dominate over what we want to remember, even when those desires are powerful.

Finally, some individuals simply have a tougher time with prospective memory than others. Over time, the resulting failures can contribute to anxiety and even obsessive-compulsive type symptoms where people excessively check back on things they've already done.[26] Anxiety, worry, and feeling driven to triple and quintuple check oneself is a pretty miserable combination, one that no doubt drains off cognitive resources that could go to better things than wondering if you turned off the coffee pot this morning.

There's no question about it: Your unaided brain is scarily unreliable when it comes to hanging onto intentions and cuing them back up at the right time. And since we don't have anything like an alarm clock in our heads, time-based intentions—those we'd like to trigger on a given date or time—are especially prone to vanishing. This applies not just to long-term recurring events like birthdays, but also to tasks that unfold over the scale of minutes.

This is a perfect case of technology excelling at something that our brains do not. The lowliest smartphone is brilliant at filing away that reminder to pick up a birthday bouquet for your significant other on the way home from work, and you can count on it to make that reminder pop up at precisely the planned moment. For the smartphone-opposed, there are also email reminders, which may not be as good at grabbing your attention and pestering you until you respond, but will jog your memory on the right day when you need to take action. Tech is also a great place to keep checklists, which happen to be another highly effective weapon in the fight against distraction-induced forgetting.[27]

Technology's power to supplement our fallible memory for intentions is something that tech advocates have touted since before the iPhone was a gleam in Steve Jobs' eye.[28] And yet, even heavy smartphone users don't always use all of its capabilities in this realm. As with so many memory-supplementing systems as well, the key may be not just to use them, but to use them consistently. I've set up a recurring reminder, for example, that serves as a sort of preflight checklist of what I need to do before my larger classes. It not only saves me from forgetting to do things like load videos or pass out worksheets, but also helps me redirect my mental capacity toward more important, cognitively demanding activities like talking to students or refreshing myself on the day's material.

Our students can benefit from these kinds of strategies as well. It's an area where instead of just forbidding phones and complaining about tech-dependence, we can open a conversation about the up sides. Try asking your students for their own tips for using tech-based memory aids like reminders and calendar alerts. And if your students prefer paper planners, ask them why, and listen carefully to what they have to say. The point isn't to criticize or convert, but rather to spark reflection on the systems we use to manage our lives and how to tailor those for maximum impact.

Those organizing systems, after all, are only getting more important as college inexorably moves away from a full-time model anchored to a consistent schedule of weekly face-to-face class meetings. With more students combining higher learning with work, raising children, and other major undertakings, the juggling act becomes more complicated. The design of the courses they are taking is also becoming less predictable and more complicated to manage. This isn't a bad thing necessarily, especially when the reasons for the complexity have to do with bringing in good practices like options to take multiple pathways through the material, flexible deadlines, and lots of small-stakes formative assignments in place of big-ticket, infrequent tests and papers. But such a slate of requirements creates a bigger load of tasks to stay on top of than even the best prospective memory could handle. We owe it to our students to let them know that human memory for this kind of thing is fallible, but that technology—when used in the right way—can help.

Talking to Students About Technology: Distraction, Learning, and the Attention Matters! Project

Clearly, there are some upsides to the complicated relationship between technology, attention, and memory. However, the downsides are also substantial. They include something that has generated more press than almost any other issue in classroom teaching over the last ten years or so: students diverted by their technology when they're supposed to be learning.

The debate may be a timely one, but inattentive students are nothing new. This is one of many astute points raised in a recent book titled *Distracted: Why Students Can't Focus and What You Can Do About It*.[29] In it, teaching expert James Lang (who is also the series editor for this book) draws on his decades of classroom experience combined with a historical take on the issue. He points out that scholars through the ages have lamented the inability of today's students—in whatever century "today" might happen to be—to resist the temptation to pay attention to anything besides what they are supposed to be studying.

Indeed, it's worth remembering that ever since the invention of the window, students have had an enticing alternative to focusing on whatever is going on inside the classroom. Lang, in *Distracted*, quotes the 17th century poet John Donne lamenting how sidetracked he became simply by watching spiders spinning webs and lizards stalking flies as he was trying to write.[30] There's always some appealing diversion to serious intellectual work, it seems. But I think that we can all appreciate that windows and spider webs, entertaining though they are, pale in comparison to the 47 notifications that have accumulated on your social media platform of choice, news of the world pouring in from every portal, and the dozen emoji-laden texts that just came in from your mom. These intrusions—relentless, frequent, and bursting with engineered urgency—kick the distraction game up to a whole new level.

Lang cites some stunning findings on just how frequently today's students succumb to the pull of their devices. In one survey, fewer than 5% of college students reported that they rarely or never strayed off-task with their phones in a normal day of classes; typically, students said they engaged in this kind of off-task activity around eleven times a day. Texting in class was a particularly common one, something my research partners and I have also found in our own surveys of undergraduates.[31] All of these findings fit with the perceptions of many teachers who say they feel that every minute in class is a competition for the attention of their perpetually wired students, and that this is a competition they are not set up to win.

Today we also have data showing exactly what happens to learning when students are digitally distracted. The news is not good. Education researcher Reynol Junco has published what I think is the most definitive data-driven takedown of technology's impacts on academic achievement, a line of research that backs up what many anti-tech educators have suspected all along. In a series of studies conducted before young people abandoned the now-frumpy Facebook platform in favor of Instagram, TikTok, and the like, Junco found that heavier Facebook users had significantly lower college grades,[32] and were less engaged in school overall.[33]

There is no shortage of explanations for these effects. If students are texting while they're studying or even while they are physically sitting in class, they are probably experiencing the kind of attentional diversion that disrupts learning, dozens or perhaps hundreds of times per day. Students who are heavily into social media are probably adding even more of these costly task-switching breaks throughout the day. Even when they're not actually checking their feeds, for social media addicts, just *thinking* about that feed might be taking up cognitive resources. This seems especially plausible when we think back to those studies showing that even when teens don't take phones to bed, their social media driven preoccupations can still disrupt sleep. And on top of everything else, it may be that students who allow these distractions to dominate study are less committed to or excited about their own educations to begin with. Even if the cause-and-effect runs in that reverse direction, it demonstrates that technology is part of a dynamic of disengagement.

As with many social science findings, this trend might seem completely obvious in hindsight: Of *course* texting all the way through your classes is going to shave points off of your grades. Of *course* students who live life on Facebook are going to care less about connecting to their school communities. But before we file this under "duh, what else would you expect?," let's remember that for quite a while there was a school of thought, enthusiastically embraced by many in higher education as well as the younger demographic themselves, that attributed special cognitive powers to people who grew up in the era of ubiquitous technology. This "digital natives" theory made the rounds for a few years, with the notion being that the technology-saturated formative experiences of this generation altered their cognitive capacities in fundamental ways, allowing them to deal with multiple streaming inputs all at once.[34]

Digital nativism seemed intuitive to a lot of people during its heyday. If true, it would have predicted that young people are immune from the worst consequences of multitasking and distraction. Or, it could even be that being able to interact with lots of technologies all at once would *increase* learning, since it would surround youngsters with a comforting buffer of the technology that they supposedly adored interacting with. But that heyday didn't last long. Many experts (me included)[35] piled on to this idea, shooting it down with one well-placed criticism after another.[36] Among other things, the human brain simply isn't reshaped dramatically on such a short time frame, and rewiring the brain for effortless task switching and expanding its bandwidth for conscious processing would be a major overhaul indeed.[37] While younger people might do marginally better in situations where they're juggling multiple inputs, that has a lot more to do with their more agile working memory systems than with a generational difference per se.[38]

Even young people's supposed love for all things digital tends to fall apart when you look at patterns such as preferences for paper textbooks versus e-books—where, surprisingly, paper wins even among solidly digital-native students.[39] The pandemic of 2020–2021 revealed even more glaring disparities between perceived and actual preferences. As class formats pivoted nearly overnight to remote (think Zoom classes) or traditional online (think discussion boards, videos, and web-based activities), there was hardly a collective sigh of relief from young college students. On the contrary, many expressed grief over the loss of the low-tech, face-to-face experience they'd expected to have, as well as simmering frustration with the technology itself. Far from being happy to be fully immersed in their "native" environment, many were as overwhelmed, if not more so, than the middle-aged remote workers who found themselves tossed into the digital deep end.

What this all points to is that young people aren't necessarily hooked on technology, but neither are they immune to its negative impacts on attention and learning. And these impacts are more than theoretical, judging from research linking heavier use to worse grades. So given all of this, what can teachers do to help students protect their attention—and thereby memory—from the relentless pull of distracting devices?

One strategy that's gotten a lot of press is the in-class tech ban—a rule by which classrooms become a sort of tech-free sterile zone where the devices are simply not allowed. While this might be appealing to some, it's probably not the best solution, and here's why. First of all is the effect on classroom mood and morale, and on the instructor's capacities as they now have to split their own attention between surveillance and teaching. Students themselves tend to rate these bans as ineffective, unappealing, and difficult to enforce.[40] If the ban encompasses laptops too, you are guaranteed to run into problems given that some students prefer or need to use them for note taking, and may in fact have legal accommodations entitling them to do so.[41]

The laptop note-taking issue is one we'll return to in the next chapter, given just how much this debate has dominated discussions of teaching with technology. There are other reasons not to rely on bans, though. Restrictive policies cut instructors off from productive and positive uses of personal devices, such as in-class quizzing and polling or collaborative work on shared documents. They don't work when students aren't in a traditional physical classroom but are instead participating in some form of online learning—which the majority of students will do for at least some, if not all, of their college educations, and where students are even more likely to engage in multitasking.[42] And most important to me, instructor-driven bans deprive students of an opportunity to learn to moderate their own device usage in the face of significant temptation—which is, after all, a vitally important contemporary life skill.

That idea of developing technology and attention management skills has been with me for a long time, as I've tried to develop solutions of my own. Early on in these efforts, I even developed a traveling road show of sorts that I'd present in courses where I was invited in as a guest speaker. The presentation featured demonstrations of some famous, striking attentional phenomena and follow-up discussions of what those tell us about the limited awareness we have about our own attentional processes. I'd close with tips on how to maximize learning by using focused, active strategies such as self-quizzing and retrieval practice, and invite students to describe how they would approach distraction and learning in more productive ways in the future.

My little show was a popular but not a particularly scalable way to spread these ideas to our student population. So on the suggestion of a brilliant instructional designer I know,[43] I set about turning it into an online, open-access module—something that anyone at our institution could sign up for. We christened the project *Attention Matters!*

Here is how the module works. Students at my institution usually find out about it through their professors; many of them offer extra credit for doing it. Module users begin by filling out a couple of short surveys, which do double duty as first, a way to research beliefs and practices involving attention, and second, as a way to help focus our participants on these issues before they begin. They then step through a sequence of three short units. The first two highlight the limits of attention, and just how much gets by us when we aren't focused. One of the main ways we do this is by showing short, memorable videos that are available online, then asking students to comment on them in an open discussion board.

One of our mainstays is called "The Amazing Color Changing Card Trick"[44]—a particularly well-done demonstration of a phenomenon called *change blindness*, whereby we miss changes to a scene (even drastic ones) if our attention is momentarily interrupted.[45] Another is a video made in Belgium, called "The Impossible Texting and Driving Test."[46] Essentially a prank with a purpose, this film shows student drivers as they're told that a (fictional) new law requires them demonstrate that they can drive and text at the same time. The hapless students then weave around the closed course, mowing down traffic cones as they shriek to the examiner that what they're being told to do is dangerous and totally impossible. Now, the *Attention Matters!* team and I never set out to address highway safety with this particular project. However, texting and driving turns out to be a universally relatable example of distraction, one that makes a great conversation starter with undergraduate students. (And, if it does discourage this incredibly risky form of multitasking among even a few of our students—we count that as another win.)

Throughout these discussions, we keep coming back to the links between attention, memory, and learning. Many of the students will spontaneously observe that they have no intention of wasting the considerable time and money they are investing in their educations, affirming that staying undistracted in class is a part of that plan.

This brings us to the last of the three units, which focuses on persuading students to adopt changes based on what they've seen in *Attention Matters!* Here, we try to leave students with some research-based tools to help make that happen. This is because just knowing the facts about a less-than-desirable habit isn't enough to create lasting changes to behavior (just ask any smoker, binge drinker, or yo-yo dieter). Neither is a just-do-it one-shot attempt born from a sudden flash of insight. Research on behavior change has made it quite clear that most people need a specific plan for how they'll resist temptation when things get tough. There also needs to be an authentic commitment to following through on the plan, something that can motivate you to stick to it even when temptation is high.

There might even be a social component to the kind of changes we hoped students would make. I say this because a classroom isn't only filled with students all doing their own things; students interact with and affect each other in complex and sometimes fraught ways. In the case of distraction, one student's good intentions can be easily undercut by another students not-so-good choices. This could range from seeing (and perhaps hearing) someone else who is tapping out text after text, to being trapped behind a neighbor who is watching, say, an entire season of *The Bachelorette* over the course of a semester (sadly, this is not actually a theoretical example, but rather something I learned was happening months in to one of my Introduction to Psychology classes).

To get students more fully engaged in the ideas presented in the module, we employed one of the sneakiest weapons in the psychology arsenal—the hypocrisy effect.[47] This effect persuades people to change behavior by asking them to either take a hypothetical stance on an issue or to articulate a desired point of view. Once they give a hypothetical opinion on a subject, people tend to stick to that opinion, despite the fact that it was only something they said because they were asked to do so. It's not particularly rational, but it works, as suggested by a long line of studies focusing on a variety of health-related behaviors.[48] We tapped into the hypocrisy effect by asking students to write down their plan for how they would manage distractions going forward. We also asked them, in one of the discussion boards, to talk with each other about their preferred strategies for dealing with a classmate who was being distracting. It didn't matter whether they went with a more confrontational approach (which a surprisingly large proportion did) or mellower tactics such as moving to a different seat. The point was that by having students publicly state their intentions, they would be more likely to follow through in the future.

These are all the best persuasive and informative techniques we know of—show, don't tell; get people to state an intention; let peers do as much of the persuading as possible. So has the project actually worked? In the sense of just engaging students in the discussion—the answer is a resounding yes. At the time of this writing, several *thousand* students have gone through the program at my university alone. Potentially thousands more have completed it around the country, as we've shared our materials with upward of

25 other universities. At this scale, even a tiny shift toward better practices adds up to big impact.

We've also learned a lot about the psychology of memory and attention just by paying attention to what our participants say on our surveys and in the discussions. For example, we've generated proof that people's beliefs and knowledge about these processes do bear some relationship to behaviors in the real world. The "counterproductive beliefs survey" (CBS), it turns out, is correlated to how much people say that they multitask in different real-world situations—texting in class, reading and answering email during meetings, watching videos or playing games on a smartphone at work. There's also a significant link between CBS scores and GPA, such that students who believe in more myths about memory and attention tend to have worse grades. Multitasking, too, turns out to be related to GPA. Echoing Junco's findings, students who reported texting in class more frequently tended to earn lower GPAs. Clearly, there is a complicated web of correlations between beliefs about attention and memory, the predilection for multitasking with our technology in real-world settings, and academic achievement.

And most importantly for our purposes, in a before-and-after comparison, we found that CBS scores were significantly better after completing the module. This means that students were *less* likely to say that they could learn by osmosis, *less* likely to endorse rereading as a good strategy for remembering what they're studying, and *more* likely to say that their own attentional abilities were not particularly exceptional, compared to other people's. These are all bedrock metacognitive and study-skills messages that are unwieldy to work into a typical college course, let alone get students to reliably adopt on their own.[49]

We learned a few other unexpected things about attention from those surveys. Surprisingly, there is a strong relationship between gender and counterproductive beliefs.[50] As it turns out, male students hold significantly more of these beliefs, especially in the realm of memory. In other words, men were substantially more likely to think that they could remember things through passive exposure, or that memory works like a video recording, and less likely to say that quizzing was a good way to study. Incorrect beliefs about attention and one's own exceptionalism were also more common among men. We are still figuring out the source of this gender difference. But it's important for instructors to know about as they think about which students might particularly benefit from something like *Attention Matters!* or other ways of addressing misconceptions about learning that might lead to self-defeating patterns of distraction and multitasking in class. We were heartened to see, too, that this module was about as effective in men as in other genders, suggesting that even among a group that is prone to these misconceptions, intervention can help.

There was another unexpected benefit from the project, and that is that it became a source of fresh new ideas about managing distracting technology. We started out thinking that the learning would largely be a one-way street, with us passing advice to students, but that assumption turned out to be gloriously wrong. In the discussion forums and reflection assignments, students talked about site-blocking apps—that software that lets you lock off distractions for a preset time—as well as an ingenious program we'd never heard of before, called Pocket Points.[51] It's not available everywhere, but where it is, it lets students amass points for time spent off their phones in class, points which are redeemable for tangible real-world items like rideshare and restaurant discounts. (Even my local outdoor outfitter accepts Pocket Points, and I'm waiting for the day when I walk in and see a particularly dedicated young student redeem theirs for, say, a kayak.)

Other student-generated ideas include using one browser program for work and one browser program for fun, as a subtle cue to stay on track during work time (and, I suppose, to stay out of one's work email during downtime). One participant even said that when he *really* needs to study, he puts his phone in a dropbox located outside in the yard, so that if he wants to scroll and text and whatnot, he's got to endure the bitterly cold Flagstaff night in order to do it. Besides all being solid strategies, these student-generated ideas make it very clear that young adults are in no way the uncritical, unquestioning technology addicts that they are made out to be. Digital natives or no, they've spent a lot of thought figuring out what they do and don't like about their devices, and on devising ways to own their technology rather than the other way around. Anyone who is interested in these issues would do well to listen to them, rather than lecture them.

Of course, for an educational psychologist the big question about *Attention Matters!* would be this: What's the long-term impact on students' learning? If students go through an experience like this, do they earn measurably better grades as a result? Do our *Attention Matters!* graduates actually put their phones away in class? I have to admit, we don't know. Our research team gathered data through the module itself but we haven't followed up with students to observe them as they are actually in their classes, or tried anything like a controlled experiment where we assign students in one class to complete the module and compare them to a control group. Long-term tracking of grades might reveal longer-term impacts as well, but I know from doing this kind of research for a long time that GPA is affected by so many other factors at the same time that it becomes difficult to see the relatively tiny influence of a single educational intervention—a type of signal-to-noise problem that crops up in this kind of applied research.

Even though we haven't made the case that this short intervention changes GPAs, I think there are still important takeaways for teachers, and really, for anyone who cares about distraction in a technological age. First, as in pretty much any endeavor where persuasion is the goal, it's important to make it a two-way dialogue rather than simply rattling off the risks of being on devices all the time. Students also have plenty of room to learn the basics of how attention and memory work, as evidenced by the big gains that our participants showed in our knowledge measures—and this knowledge is probably important to address in college, given the relationship between it and GPA. Male students in particular would likely benefit from this direct approach given that they are more prone to counterproductive beliefs.

All of these pieces of advice should also reinforce that one big take-away for teachers: Attention and memory can't be separated. These days, technology and attention can't be separated either, given how perfectly suited our devices are for interrupting, diverting, and engrossing us. It's what they're made to do. But this doesn't mean we, as champions of undistracted learning, should make those devices our sworn enemies. We need to stay on the right side of the issue with claims that we can support with good science, while steering away from myths and rumors fueled by clickbait culture. We also need to give our devices credit where credit is due, especially for their amazing ability to remind and cue us to follow through on actions at the right time—an underrated, but vital thing our memories are responsible for doing. And finally, we shouldn't complain about the younger generations' misconceptions about distraction and learning, unless we're also prepared to address those with good science and workable strategies.

CHAPTER SUMMARY

- Attention is a complex phenomenon that arises out of the brain's mechanisms for prioritizing the allocation of cognitive resources. It is what allows us to filter out or suppress anything that's not currently relevant, while simultaneously monitoring our surroundings for anything that could potentially be important.

- There are a number of myths and misconceptions about attention, some fueled by popular ideas about technology. These include the idea that attention spans are shrinking due to technology, that students only pay attention for ten minutes at a time in class, and that digital devices cause a specific form of burnout or fatigue within the brain.

- Attention is needed for almost all instances of new memory formation. It is particularly interrelated with prospective memory, which tends to be disrupted very easily when a person is distracted.

- In some ways, technology can help benefit highly fallible forms of memory including prospective memory. Reminders, alerts, and to-do lists all complement human cognitive capabilities particularly well.

- Digital technologies clearly have extraordinary potential to distract us, and thereby disrupt the formation of new memories.

- Research conducted as part of the *Attention Matters!* project at Northern Arizona University demonstrates that a brief, nontechnical educational module can significantly reduce counterproductive beliefs about attention and memory. Student comments gathered as part of the project also revealed a surprisingly large number of original insights about technology and distraction, counter to the popular idea that young adults are uncritically accepting of technology in their lives.

TEACHING TAKE-AWAYS

- For practical purposes, there is no such thing as passively absorbing information "by osmosis." Attention is necessary for memory, so students need to be not only physically present but also attentive in order to create new connections and acquire new knowledge.
- Consider how you'll attract and maintain students' attention at the same time as you are designing other aspects of courses and learning activities. At the same time, be aware that attempting to ban all technology during classes may not be an effective or practical strategy.
- Confronting the problem of distracted students can be difficult and demoralizing. It may help to take the long view, remembering that scholars have written about distraction and learning for centuries, and that not all of the problems are new ones.
- Be cautious about repeating or reinforcing myths about attention that students may have heard before, such as the ten-minute myth, the idea that digital natives are

different, or the idea that mobile devices are irreparably damaging human attention.

- Talking to students about the shared challenges most of us face with managing distracting technologies can reveal some surprising insights. Your students have probably already grappled with ways to stay focused both in and out of class, and can share those with you and with each other if they're invited to in the right way.

- The *Attention Matters!* project suggests that believing in myths about attention is related to dysfunctional multitasking behaviors, which in turn predict lower GPA. Targeting these mistaken beliefs can be part of helping develop your students' metacognitive skills.

- To effectively teach students to manage distracting technologies, don't stop at giving them the facts. Try also challenging them to consider how they'll stick to technology management plans, especially when they're bored, frustrated, or dealing with in-class neighbors who are distracting them.

—

CHAPTER 5

THE DEVICES WE CAN'T PUT DOWN

—

Smartphones, Laptops, Memory, and Learning

Computers started making serious inroads into our daily lives when they became portable. They seemed to meld with our very essence when they assumed the form of pocket-sized portals to the open internet. Gaming, news, urgent work communications, running to-do lists, even our entire social networks—all of those things are perpetually just one "unlock screen" away, thanks to the tiniest and most addictive technology ever invented.

Education, as a field, was relatively slow to catch on to the massive trend toward mobile and smartphone-based computing. Well into the years that saw the meteoric global rise of the iPhone, the makers of education-targeted technologies—textbook publishing firms, learning management system companies, and so on—lagged behind in making products that would even *work* on a phone, let alone take advantage of the unique affordances of these ultraportable computers. So it's not surprising that in education circles, we're still thrashing around a bit to define a coherent philosophy of what these devices mean for learning.

Furthermore, within these education circles, the discussion has overwhelmingly concentrated on the power of mobile devices to distract students, especially during face-to-face, in-person classes. Smartphones, after all, are small enough to conceal under a desk, enabling students to text their way through an entire lecture if they choose. The laptops that start out as a wonderful tool for taking notes and accessing reference materials soon morph into means to do anything except focus on class—a temptation that requires an iron will to resist once your hands are on the keyboard and your eyes are on the screen. These problems are all reminiscent of the issues addressed in the *Attention Matters!* module I talked about in the previous chapter, in that we are grappling with a very real threat to attention, and thus to learning, that students and teachers simply can't escape in the contemporary world. Taking an in-depth look at what exactly happens in our cognitive systems when we are using mobile devices, or when we're even in the mere presence of those devices, is therefore a key piece of understanding the big picture of how technology relates to learning.

Once we get into the bigger picture, it becomes clear that the implications of carrying computers around with us go beyond obvious instances of distraction. There are other kinds of subtle effects, ones that we might not notice in the moment but that over time begin to alter what we remember and how capable we are of effectively using the knowledge we acquire. These effects include our episodic memories of things we've experienced, our ability to navigate around an environment based on spatial information we've stored in memory, and even what we learn along the way as we take notes in a classroom. Today, all of these outcomes reflect the influence of the devices most of us choose to rely on to process and record information, a choice we might make with the intention of enhancing our day-to-day functioning but which sometimes creates unintended consequences.

The moral-panic strain of antitechnology rhetoric has flourished around portable devices, especially the smartphone. This constant visual, auditory, even tactile reminder of the prominence of computing in our lives naturally makes us wonder what might be happening in our minds as a result. Like tiny, annoying lightning rods, smartphones seem to attract and concentrate people's negative perceptions about technology—that it has become intrusive, is inescapable, and is changing us for the worse.

The panic crowd is clearly right about one thing—smartphones are a new ballgame in terms of potential influences on our cognitive processes. As the psychologist Henry Wilmer and colleagues put it in a meaty review of research on the subject, "smartphones are an especially impactful technological development, due to their flexibility of function, portability, and increasing proliferation."[1] According to these authors, the thoroughness with which smartphones have permeated our contemporary lives actually makes them somewhat difficult to study in controlled fashion, because it's now essentially impossible to study control groups of individuals who don't use these devices at all.

This difficulty is compounded by the fact that so many studies use self-report questionnaires as their main form of measurement. At this point in history, most adults have been exposed to the idea that smartphones are hazardous to one's cognitive health. This exposure could create subtle expectations that people unconsciously hew to in their answers—a self-fulfilling prophecy of sorts. There's also the fact that, as with many behaviors involving time, people are just not that accurate at estimating how frequently they use their phones.[2] More objective measures, such as examining people's cognitive performance in different domains and correlating those with actual observed patterns of phone use, would skirt around these problems. But these kinds of direct measurements are complicated and time-consuming to gather, and thus, we're often stuck with a person's own, potentially distorted, perceptions of how their phones might be affecting them.

Even given these limitations, though, there are a few things researchers can confidently conclude about what phones do and don't do to our minds. Much as we saw with the questions having to do with attention and computing in general, the relationship between phones and mental functioning isn't a clear-cut case of degradation and impairment.

Neural and Cognitive Consequences of Using Smartphones

One study, conducted by the psychologist P. Andrew Leynes and colleagues, used a technique called event-related potentials to pinpoint what happens to mental processes, at a neural level, as a function of regular smartphone use.[3]

Event-related potentials, or "ERPs", are tiny fluctuations in electrical activity that can be picked up through electrodes placed on the outside of the scalp. These fluctuations reflect the activity of groups of cells within the brain. Researchers are usually interested in tracking what happens to this activity as a function of some stimulus they present—namely, something research subjects are seeing, hearing, or doing. This is the "event-related" part of the terminology. Over the years, ERP researchers have built up enough data about these event-related responses that they can reliably identify patterns that are associated with different cognitive processes, such as processing visual material or picking up on anomalous words within sentences. ERP methodology can even detect certain kinds of interior mental reactions, such as surprise or boredom.

Leynes' research team was interested in comparing these telltale ERP signatures across experienced and naive smartphone users as they completed a task involving divided attention across a phone and a reading task. So how did they get around the problem that there are so few phone-naive individuals left to study? Ingeniously, the team took advantage of a previously existing data set that had collected the same kind of measurements, from the same type of research subjects, back in 2007—before smartphones had achieved the total domination of the planet that they have now.

When the researchers compared these older data with data from present-day heavy phone users, they found that ERP responses associated with visual-spatial processing were reduced in the experienced group, relative to the naive group. Cognitively speaking, this reduced neural response is actually a good thing, because it means that the brain isn't working as hard to process visual data. Granted, this is a single study, and as the researchers acknowledge, there could be other differences across the two cohorts that could possibly account for the differences. However, it's one thought-provoking example of how smartphones might be creating across-the-board changes within the brain—and as it happens in this case, the changes were positive.

Visual-spatial processing is certainly important, but it's not what most of us mean when we think about the mental processes that power learning. In an effort to target this kind of higher-order cognitive processing, another study targeted thinking style. This is an important choice given that so many of the concerns commonly voiced among technology skeptics involve thinking abilities, broadly defined. Specifically, the researchers set out to test the claim that smartphones encourage poor thinking habits and practices. These included superficial skimming, jumping to conclusions, and avoiding deep engagement with challenging topics. In other words, the researchers wanted to know: As phones get smarter, do their users get dumber?

Researchers tried to approach this question directly by looking at the correlation between degree of smartphone use—heavy or light—and the ability to reason.[4] After asking study volunteers about their typical phone use, researchers presented them with a set of notoriously challenging logic problems. What makes these logic problems so hard isn't the complexity (many contain just a few key pieces of information), or the need for some kind of special expertise. It's that the problems dangle a tempting-but-wrong answer that seems obvious unless you go through some difficult, precise mental calculations.

Take this famous example, one that gets under my skin every time I see it: "A bat and a ball cost $1.10 in total. The bat costs $1.00 more than the ball. How much does the ball cost?" (Hint: Not ten cents.[5]) Questions like this one reveal how carefully and deliberately you tend to think.

The prediction was that heavy smartphone users would be more prone to zipping straight to obvious answers, and that conversely, lighter users would be willing and able to engage in deeper, more difficult forms of thought. This is exactly what the analyses revealed: a correlation between level of smartphone use and cognitive style, in favor of the lighter users. Notably, the overall amount of time spent online didn't have this same predictive relationship—rather, it was specific to smartphones. The particular kinds of activities that volunteers used their smartphones for also mattered. Those who more frequently used their phones to conduct searches were especially predisposed toward the less-deliberative, shortcutting cognitive style. Heavier use of phones for entertainment and social media, by contrast, mattered less.

This last finding is what the researchers zeroed in on to argue that they had found another case of the offloading dynamic, the one commonly implicated as one mechanism by which technology affects information processing. Like the study about online searching described in chapter 3, where people tended not to encode information in memory if they believed they could look it up later, these results suggest that constantly going to your phone for answers makes you less willing and able to work out the answers on your own. The finding also highlights yet another link between thinking and memory. Searching out information, rather than relying on one's stored knowledge, might be part of an overall pattern of thinking in which speed and ease are prioritized over accuracy.

That is the story that the study's authors would like to tell, and they do make a good case for it. But there are multiple caveats we need to consider before concluding that researchers have found the smoking gun implicating smartphones in the untimely death of human cognitive capabilities. This study, like most, used self-report for the heavy-use measurement, so we can't be sure that the relationship involved actual use versus any of the factors that might influence our perception of use—among which is simply the shoddy memory we have of such everyday minutiae.

Furthermore, given that the study was set up to look at correlations between preexisting variables instead of assigning people to control groups and so forth, we simply can't be sure about the direction of cause and effect. It could easily be the case that people who already lean toward a superficial cognitive style are attracted to the ease of searching on their phones. Or, there could be an unknown third factor—a personality quirk, some demographic characteristic—that influences both of these outcomes, in parallel.

Both of these are plausible alternatives to the possibility that habitually using your phone to look up information causes alterations to your thinking style. I'll grant, though, that this study presents a red flag about the possibility that it does. Perhaps it provides one more reason not to rely exclusively on Google instead of our own memories, even when we can.

So, phone use might alter our minds with respect to a few fundamental aspects of cognitive processing. Still, there's still scant evidence that they're wreaking havoc across the board. Given that, we can look more closely at some impacts that are specifically true for memory. To do that, we should begin by going back to memory's most important precursor: attention.

Smartphones and Attention

The key affordance of smartphones—the thing that sets them apart from other computing devices that came before them—is that they stay with you, on your person or within reach. Tied up with this barnacle-like ability to stick with us is their constant communicative function. Notifications pull us away from what we're doing with fiendish efficiency. And even when we've suppressed the pings, badges, and other obvious interruptions, phones provide constant visual reminders of all the engrossing things we can do with them. It's an attention disaster waiting to happen.

This brings us to one of the most unsettling studies on phones and attention that's come along in some time. It's not one that looks at how distracting it is to receive notifications, or how ill-advised it is to try to multitask while our eyes and brain are glued to the device. None of those impacts are that surprising, and by now they are well documented in the research literature. Instead, this experiment looked at how distracting a phone can be even when we aren't using it, listening to it, or even holding it in our hands.

A team led by psychologist Bill Thornton presented research volunteers with a set of timed pencil-and-paper tests designed to take intense concentration to complete. These included tasks like searching and crossing out specific numbers from a row of numbers, doing the same for sequences of numbers that added up to a specific number (e.g., if your target number is 3, cross out 2 1), and drawing lines between an array of numbered circles in correct order. The researchers subtly manipulated one aspect of the testing situation, like this: For one randomly assigned group of volunteers, the research assistant administering the test casually placed her cell phone on the edge of the table before the tests began. For the control group, the research assistant placed a cellphone-sized spiral notebook in the same spot.

That one tweak to the situation did in fact affect how well participants did on the attention-demanding tasks. At the easier levels of the tests—for example, just finding and crossing off single numbers—there wasn't a difference. But as the tests got harder—crossing off numbers that add to a target number, dealing with circles that were labeled with *either* numbers or letters, in order—performance got worse in the presence of the phone. Researchers interpreted this pattern as evidence that just that one environmental cue—someone else's phone sitting off in the periphery—can grab our attention, enough to matter when we're engaged in a particularly demanding activity.

That's enough to give one pause, and perhaps cause one to reconsider the habit of leaving phones around in any old place when we're trying to get work done. It's sobering to think that phones have acquired enough power over us, at a deep enough level of our consciousness, that we can't help but divert our focus toward them.

That said, there are a few caveats we have to apply to this study as well. On the one hand, the design was experimental, not correlational, meaning that we don't have to worry that we're comparing across two groups of volunteers who might differ in some fundamental way (e.g., that there's a certain kind of person who chooses to be around phones, since volunteers weren't given the choice but rather were randomly assigned to the groups). On the other hand, like most well-controlled experiments, Thornton's procedure was a bit contrived. For example, the phone in question was someone else's, not one's own phone as we would most commonly be dealing with in a real-life situation involving distraction.

There have been some questions as well about how consistently this effect shows up; not all studies attempting to replicate the effect have been able to do so.[6] Strangely, one of these replication studies found that when you substitute a person's *own* phone into the procedure, and have them either keep their phones in view or set them in another room, they tend to rate the tasks they are doing in the experiment as easier and less boring.[7] This turns out to be especially true for people who describe themselves as more attached to their phones. This suggests (but doesn't confirm definitively) that the phone-dependent among us are in a bit of a catch-22. Having our phones in view while we try to work is distracting, but so is being separated from them altogether.

The notion that smartphones are uniquely distracting, even when we aren't actively poking away at them, also fits with the findings of another line of research. A team of researchers led by psychologist Cary Stothart investigated how distracting it was to receive notifications on your phone even when you don't have any intention of answering them. Researchers engaged participants in a computer-based vigilance task that allowed them to pinpoint any lapse in attention that happened. Then, in an ingenious twist, researchers arranged to send notifications (unbeknown to the research volunteers) that were audible during the procedure. The volunteers, believing that they were hearing real notifications, saw their performance crash, compared to how they had done in an undistracted state—even though none actually responded. The team speculated—plausibly, I think—that this performance drop-off happened because of the volley of off-topic thoughts triggered with each new ring and ping.

One last reason to credit smartphones with a unique ability to distract us comes from that same study by Leynes and colleagues on the event-related potentials associated with receiving notifications. Even though these researchers found that smartphone use was associated with improvements to the efficiency of visual processing, in a different study, they found some powerful physical evidence of how distracting it can be to interact with phones. It turns out there's also an electrical signature associated with noticing information that's relevant to an ongoing task, a signal that's easily picked up with the ERP technique. This telltale brainwave pattern was reduced by around *fifty percent* in participants who were using a smartphone to do the experimental task. This is one sobering way to quantify the size of the impact, and it drives home the idea that these kinds of effects aren't just subjective impressions, but instead are rooted deeply in our brains' attentional mechanisms.

Let's acknowledge again that none of these studies demonstrated long-term, lasting erosion of anybody's attentional capabilities. The negative effects they revealed were primarily short-term decrements, impacts that go away when the phone does. But they all give a new perspective on what many of us have long suspected: Smartphones are wildly distracting.

One of the reasons we care so much about the distraction wrought by smartphones is because being distracted undercuts memory. What are some other ways that smartphones can directly affect what and how well we remember?

One possibility is that smartphones magnify the "I can Google it later" effect we encountered in a previous chapter—the one where believing that you'll be able to search for information leads you not to encode it as well in your own memory.[8] That finding was a general one having to do with any kind of access to information stored digitally, but it seems likely that smartphones could increase this tendency even further. Because people tend to keep their phones with them constantly, and use them so frequently, phones accentuate that sense that we can just rely on search engines for everything we need to know. Right now, this link is only hypothetical—but it's highly plausible given what we already know.

Other research has attempted to pinpoint impacts of

specific uses for smartphones, especially those that affect our memory for experiences as we move through different physical environments. In this case, the relevant kind of memory is *episodic* memory, meaning impressions connected to firsthand experiences we had in particular places. It's an apt choice, given the contemporary trend toward using our phones throughout all kinds of excursions, both to take photos and to share what we're experiencing with others via social media and messaging. These memories are also the kind that we tend to be particularly interested in creating and preserving, whether it's because they're so enjoyable, or because (for example, in the case of a field trip or work event) the purpose is to gather information we will need later on.

So does using your phone during a real-world experience affect what you remember about that experience? Here, we probably want to count as a given the fact that if you're simply distracted with off-topic tasks and notifications the whole time, you'll encode less. More interesting are questions about how attempting to record the experience itself changes recall. This was the subject of an experiment by Diana Tamir and colleagues, who set out to discover what happens when we use a phone to record something we're experiencing, and also, what happens when we're intent on sharing the experience on social media.

Tamir's research team asked volunteers to tour a local landmark,[9] and later tested what they remembered about the place they visited. This memory test was a surprise, so that just like with real-world memories, participants weren't deliberately trying to memorize details along the way. It also took place after a solid delay—at least one week after the tour—which also helped make the test as realistic as possible. To simulate the effect of using a cellphone camera, researchers assigned some volunteers to use devices to take photos along the way. Volunteers were further subdivided into two groups, one that was asked to take pictures for their own use and one that was asked to share the photos on social media immediately after the tour. Those assigned to the control condition left their cellphones behind before embarking on the tour.

The results of the camera–no camera comparison were quite clear: People who took pictures remembered less. This applied regardless of whether the photos were for personal use or for online sharing. What wasn't as clear were the reasons for this difference. Other measurements taken after the visit showed no differences in engagement, enjoyment, or feelings of being present during the experience itself. But even if they didn't nail down the precise reasons for the effect, the researchers did find solid evidence that, ironically enough, the devices we use to hang onto cherished experiences actually degrade the memories we have of those experiences.

Is there a way out of this catch-22? Older research on the psychology of photographing scenes suggests that there may be. Psychologist Linda Henkel assigned research volunteers to do something similar to the procedure in the landmark-tour experiment.[10] Participants toured a museum exhibit with instructions to photograph certain objects, and not to photograph other objects. On a surprise memory test later on, objects that people had taken pictures of weren't remembered as well as objects that volunteers had simply examined without taking any photos. This pattern seems like another argument for the memory-destroying effects of snapping pictures, except for a twist discovered in a follow-up study: When people are told to take pictures of specific *parts* of objects—for example, just the hands of a statue—memory is almost as good as when they are taking no pictures at all.

On the one hand, this could seem like a minuscule exception to an overall trend—and who, after all, would really spend their time during a memorable experience worrying about the finer points of photographing whole things or just parts? But that would miss the real point of the part-versus-whole finding, which is this: Being attentive counteracts the photo-offloading effect. In other words, when we're focused more intently on the experience—as we would be when selecting specific things to photograph—that focus kick-starts the process of forming new memories of what we're doing. That offsets the costs associated with being distracted by taking the picture, as well as the decrements caused by offloading the memory from our brains to our photographs.

All in all, the impacts of picture-taking on memory should remind us of the multistage, multidimensional nature of memory, and how different stages of creating and accessing memories can be affected differently by the presence of technology. Successfully remembering an experience requires multiple things to go exactly right. We have to encode the information in the first place, which in turn requires that we are not only attentive, but also that we take some level of responsibility for remembering it ourselves rather than assuming we can rely on an external mechanism. Then, we need to be able to get that encoded information back out of storage, usually with the aid of some kind of a cue. And with that, we need to give credit to external recordings for providing excellent cues. As Henkel points out in her article, there's plenty of research showing that examining a photograph can trigger and effectively reactivate details from our own memories, which makes them a wonderful complement to our own memories.

In the end, what should we believe about our memories and smartphone cameras—and as importantly, what should we do differently in light of the research? There's good reason, on the front end, to be careful about spending too much time during an important experience taking pictures. We can shoot just the most important or irresistible details, and when we do, we can stop and focus on what specific details we're attempting to capture. More subtly, we can alter our mindset about what cellphone photos are for, from a memory standpoint. Ideally, we create these pictures not as an easy substitute for our own recollections, but as a way to trigger those recollections later on.

It's reminiscent of a compromise approach that I heard about from one group of my own young-adult students. On a big trip they'd planned to celebrate their senior year, these young women made a pact not to use their phones to take pictures, instead choosing to use disposable cameras to record just a few choice shots along the way. This arrangement both forced the group members to be more selective about what they chose to photograph, while heading off the inevitable distractions that suck you in when you pull your phone out to capture that gorgeous sunset or perfect selfie.

These students' deliberate approach offers some encouraging points for teachers as well. It's another reminder that our students themselves are a source of ideas for managing memory when technology is involved, and that not all young people feel the need to be yoked to their phones at all times. All of the research, taken together, offers other insights for teachers who take on the labor-intensive, important work of setting up experiences like field trips and site visits. It likely makes sense to raise the issue with students ahead of time, setting expectations and norms for phone cameras, or perhaps for when phones should be out at all. The research also provides relatable examples of the important principles linking memory and attention, as well as how seemingly small changes—like taking pictures of partial objects—can have a big impact when they tap into those principles.

Similarly, there's another line of research based on real-world activities that we can tie in to principles that matter for learning. This research grows out of an established body of work on the effects of GPS-style navigation on memory for spatial environments, something that used to be done by dedicated navigation devices but that's now typically handled by a phone. The question here is: Does using a phone to get detailed directions as we move through a region in space hinder the process of learning how to get around that region on our own? And if so, is that negative impact any worse than it would be for low-tech alternatives like paper maps?

According to one early study of this issue, the answers are yes and yes.[11] Using a driving simulator, researchers asked volunteers to make their way through a virtual town, aided either by paper maps or GPS-style turn-by-turn directions. When they were later presented with a surprise recall test, volunteers in the turn-by-turn group showed poorer recall, with sparser mental maps and a decreased ability to sketch important landmarks.

Research since then has offered more evidence that over time, using navigation aids slows down the formation of our own knowledge, resulting in longer and less efficient trips (especially when the aids are taken away).[12] There may even be a rich-get-richer effect here too, because people who perceive themselves to be less adept at navigation are especially likely to rely on computer-generated directions, which then causes them to store even less information that might help them navigate in the future.[13] This phenomenon both offers caution about relying on phones to get around environments that we'd like to develop a better understanding of, and puts another checkmark in the column of mental processes that can deteriorate as a function of offloading.

In sum, phones probably do affect what we remember as we use them in typical ways—taking pictures, getting directions, and searching for information. They almost certainly affect memory when they do what they do best—send attention-grabbing alerts that cause us to disengage from what we're supposed to be doing. This power in particular may be something phones exert over us even when we're separated from them, or even reminded in some way of their existence. The jury is still out on whether heavy phone use degrades our ability to use knowledge in more profound ways, but if it does, that would constitute another part of the same familiar dynamic, one in which phones encourage us to over-rely on them, perhaps combined with their ability to train us to like and expect instant results.

Should We Try to Give Up Mobile Devices— or At Least Curtail Them?

Given the risks to memory and perhaps thought itself, should teachers make it their mission to separate students from their ever-present phones? Should we *all* be separating ourselves from mobile devices, just to be on the safe side?

The answer, I think, is "only partly," and here is why. First, I think that phones have a lot to offer in terms of reinforcing weaker areas of cognition. In the previous chapter, I talked about the problem of prospective memory, something that brains are awful at but where phones excel, and in the next chapter, we'll look at how technology can serve an assistive function to those of us facing specific individual challenges. Second, teachers would be missing out on good educational applications I described in an earlier chapter—the Duolingos, the Kahoots, and (hopefully) even better incarnations of technology to come. Used strategically and well, these smartphone-friendly apps are a boon to students, and so passing up on all of them is a heavy tradeoff.

Third, and finally, as we weigh those tradeoffs, there is the encouraging fact that we can mitigate some of the issues once we really understand why they are happening, from the inside out. One thing that jumps out after a close look at the research is that the problems with smartphones aren't an inevitability, or something inherent to the machines themselves. Instead, all of them trace back to particular ways we use the devices (or allow ourselves to be used by them, as the case may be). Once we see and understand the ways in which our cognitive processes are being pulled off track, we can effectively resist.

This blind spot, where we pin problems on the devices without considering why the problems happen, is nowhere more evident than in a long-running debate over another type of device that has made enormous inroads into daily life: the laptop. Specifically, the debate focuses on the note-taking students do in class and what the cognitive implications are for using laptops, and not paper, for this purpose.

Should Teachers Let Students Take Notes on Laptops?

The question about using laptops for taking notes has fired up more heated opinions than nearly any other topic in technology and teaching in the last ten years. Rarely do the finer points of higher education pedagogy make it into the popular consciousness, but this one did, in spectacular fashion. Over a period spanning several years, multiple op-eds in major magazines and newspapers[14] argued that laptops are hazardous to learning, usually concluding that teachers ought to simply forbid these devices during class.

This explosion of interest then touched off a counter-reaction, in the form of a flurry of articles and blog posts[15] from nationally known teaching experts, most of whom took the opposite stance on the wisdom of forbidding laptops in class. Writers in this camp argued that blanket bans have some serious downsides and warned against over-extension of the fairly limited research evidence against laptop-based notetaking.

Regarding that research evidence, virtually everybody cites one particular series of experiments that was reported in a 2014 article by the cognitive psychologists Pam Mueller and Daniel Oppenheimer. This article carried the catchy (for an academic journal, anyway) title "The Pen Is Mightier Than the Keyboard: Advantages of Longhand Over Laptop Note Taking," and to this day it remains the weapon of choice for anyone who wants to argue the case for handwriting over keyboarding in education. As one research team observed about the study, "It has also captured the academic imagination; as of January 15, 2021, Mueller and Oppenheimer (2014) have been cited more than 1,100 times (Google Scholar), and the article's Attention score places it in 'the top 5% of all research outputs ever tracked by Altmetric.'"[16]

In this study, Mueller and Oppenheimer set out to examine the impact, on memory specifically, of taking handwritten notes versus keyboarding in situations that are similar to a college classroom. Their research volunteers were asked to watch a 15-minute recorded TED talk, a format that the researchers believed to be roughly similar to that of an in-class lecture. Volunteers were told to take notes using their usual techniques, and here's where the critical variable came into play. Some were randomly assigned to use paper notebooks, and others were assigned to use laptops (not their own, but ones provided by researchers, on which internet access was disabled to prevent off-topic activities during the experiment).

After watching the talks, volunteers were led off to another room where they engaged in some demanding working-memory tasks for about a half hour. This way, researchers could be sure that they'd wiped out any short-term recollection of the talks before testing volunteers over what they remembered. The test questions paralleled what many faculty do in real exams, in that there were different levels and kinds of questions. Some questions focused on factual recall and others focused on conceptual relationships—items requiring prediction, comparison, application, and the like.

Researchers didn't just look at test performance. They also analyzed the notes themselves, to get a sense of how the two forms of note taking differ, focusing on important variables such as the overall amount of verbiage written and the degree to which there was verbatim transcription of what the TED speakers had said. This way, they could test the common assertion that note-takers don't work as hard to condense and synthesize what they're hearing when they can quickly copy down exactly what's being said. If this is the case, there should be a less-is-more phenomenon, whereby the slower process of handwriting induces more complex thought, and thus better memorability, according to the well-documented depth of processing effect.

The results of this comparison told a powerful story about the link between note-taking modality, memory, and what people tend to write when they're using different mechanisms for doing so. There was a clear and significant advantage for longhand note taking in the case of conceptual recall questions. Factual questions, by contrast, were little affected by how people took notes. When taking handwritten notes, the research volunteers wrote less, but what they wrote also overlapped less with the text of the TED talks, such that there did appear to be a lower level of verbatim transcription and a greater amount of concise, originally worded summary of the content in handwritten notes. And, it turned out that the less verbatim overlap there was in a given set of notes, the better the performance was on the memory test.

The bottom line: Results were consistent with the intuitions of many laptop skeptics, confirming that people write more and remember less when keyboarding.

The work certainly *sounds* like the last word in favor of low-tech note taking. And as a researcher, I'd agree that the design and execution of the study are, if not flawless, very strong. In particular, the authors did a tremendous job drawing precise comparisons among different kinds of exam questions and digging deeply into the finer points of how different methods of note taking affect what we capture. But as with any single study that's expected to support major changes to our teaching practices—or even changes to our overall acceptance of laptops in daily life—we have to look in depth at what that study did well, what it didn't do as well, and what it ultimately can and can't tell us.

It's also important to determine whether the same results are likely to happen under different circumstances. To do this, the gold standard is replication—in other words, having other researchers try the same procedure to see if they get the same outcomes. We social science researchers don't do nearly as much replication as we should, but in the case of the laptop study, several complete replications have now been carried out, and the results are eye-opening.[17]

For one replication, researchers Kayla Morehead, John

Dunlosky, and Katherine A. Rawson first did exactly what Mueller and Oppenheimer did, randomly assigning different groups of volunteers to use different methods of note taking while watching the same exact set of TED talks, then testing what they remembered afterward.[18] This time, the team did *not* find a significant advantage of handwriting for the conceptual questions, although strangely they did find such an advantage in the case of purely factual questions. The original pattern of a greater volume of notes being taken via laptop held up in the replication, with volunteers writing more and including more verbatim transcription when using laptops.

In other words, some patterns found in the original study replicated, but some—most notably the conceptual recall question advantage—did not. When findings like this can't be reproduced consistently, naturally it raises questions about why that is, and unfortunately, we can't tell for sure based on the Morehead team's study alone. It may be that the effect is simply more fragile, more subject to change with any tiny alteration to context, than it originally appeared to be. As social scientists have pointed out about all kinds of replications, when you're looking at differences that are fairly subtle to begin with, you may not be able to observe them in every single sample, even when all the correct procedures are in place and there's nothing questionable about the original study. Random variations in the characteristics of your sample, your testing conditions and so on can obscure the view of smaller, less dramatic effects. This is consistent with the fact that the larger, more dramatic of the effects found in the original study—the differences in the number of words written and the level of verbatim transcription—held up just fine in the replication.

All this back and forth is good social science, but from a practical standpoint it leads to one fairly glaring conclusion: If the supposed advantage of handwriting is subtle enough, or simply small enough, not to reliably show up across studies, we probably shouldn't be remaking our classroom policies because of it. We should also set a much higher bar for any future op-ed pieces singing the praises of handwriting, with the expectation that the authors will need to offer either some major caveats based on the replication question, or a good explanation for why these newer findings don't matter. That alone would be a huge contribution of the Morehead replication study: reintroducing nuance and reminding us that one study does not a definitive scientific conclusion make.

This wasn't the only contribution of the replication study, though, and it's important that some of the researchers' additional insights not get lost in the back-and-forth over the laptop question. As a carefully planned extension to the original Mueller and Oppenheimer procedure, the team also looked at another technology for taking notes: eWriters. These note-taking tools are digital, but don't involve keyboarding. Instead, they are designed to mimic the experience of writing on paper, but with a tablet-type interface. eWriters offer a paper-saving alternative to physical notebooks, and although at the time of this writing they haven't taken off in terms of popularity, Morehead and colleagues make a good case that if we care about the impact of different technologies on memories for what we write, we should expand the range of technologies that we're looking at. eWriters also offer a way to tease apart the impact of using a technological aid per se from any effects that are due to keyboarding. Overall, their findings showed that eWriters produced similar patterns as writing on paper, both with respect to the word count and verbatim overlap, as well as the impact (or lack thereof) on memory for the content of the notes.

The replication study team also brought up a major issue in the interpretation of the findings, one that ought to make us step back and take a new perspective on the overall question of how notes help students learn. This interpretation issue goes back to the idea of students' learning as a function of creating the notes—in other words, acquiring knowledge right then and there while they are writing. This is termed the *encoding function* of notes. But as the researchers pointed out in the write-up of the replication study, this isn't the only way that notes promote learning. Typically, class notes have their bigger impact later on, while students are going back and reviewing what they wrote. This is the *storage function* of notes, and here, it's not the modality or even the amount of notes that matter, but the relevance of what was written down to the eventual exam, quiz, or other assessment of learning.

The storage function of notes always strikes me as less exciting than the encoding function, and that might be why it is rarely mentioned in antilaptop editorials. It's just something you'd assume is part of studying—deliberately sitting down and putting in the effort to review and refresh on what you heard. The encoding function, on the other hand, offers the promise of learning without even reviewing. And while this function is important—and indeed, although memories are formed all the time without deliberate review and rehearsal—learning while taking notes still seems like a side benefit, something that is a nice bonus but not what most students are depending on to get prepared for a test. Morehead and colleagues don't write about it specifically, but there is the additional possibility that good notes can be the basis for even more powerful study techniques, such as retrieval practice or relating the material to your own life. These techniques, too, would work best when a students' notes are comprehensive, accurate, and relevant.

Put another way, the real bread and butter function of notes might not be the cool side effect of creating memories while writing, but rather, in supporting effective studying later on. So how does the quality of notes fit into the laptop versus handwriting question? Morehead and colleagues looked at characteristics of notes taken by their research volunteers, defining quality along two dimensions: first, how many test answers happened to be included in the notes (i.e., relevance), and how many concepts were incorporated as a function of how many words were written (i.e., efficiency). The idea here is that notes that have a dense concentration of conceptual material, and are well-aligned with the content of the eventual test, will be particularly useful for studying.

The team compared these quality measures across modes of note taking and found no differences in the relevance and efficiency of notes taken by the three methods. Nor did they find significant differences in test performance when volunteers were allowed to study their notes before the test (a variation that would enhance any effect associated with the storage function), although there was a nonsignificant trend toward *better* performance for the laptop group.

Morehead and colleagues ended their article by stating that based on the research, there simply isn't enough evidence to justify prescribing one method of note taking over another, and I quite agree. Also, if you go back to the original "pen is mightier than the keyboard" study, those authors themselves include numerous qualifications to their conclusion that teachers ought to prescribe handwritten notes. Most notably, they point out that laptops are going to be a problem mainly *if* note-takers use them to "indiscriminately" transcribe reams of undigested lecture content. In other words, we shouldn't look on laptops in general with suspicion, but rather, focus on note-taking techniques.

These observations jibe with an even more recent replication attempt, this one conducted by Tufts University professor Heather Urry and a student research team.[19] Urry's group reran the original Mueller and Oppenheimer study with scrupulous attention to keeping almost every detail the same, right down to showing the identical set of TED talks to their research volunteers. Once again, this study did replicate the core finding that people do in fact write more when taking notes by laptop, and that they score lower on retention tests when their notes contain a high degree of verbatim overlap with the talk they're watching. However, handwritten notes failed to produce any appreciable improvement in performance, either for conceptual or factual-style exam questions.

Across multiple studies, then, a similar pattern is emerging: When studied under controlled experimental conditions, the advantages of longhand writing are inconsistent at best, and nonexistent at worst. Verbatim transcription does seem to lower exam performance, but as Urry's team points out, there is another important caveat to interpreting this connection as straight cause and effect. It may be the case that students who are more likely to engage in transcription-style note taking are less conscientious, less motivated or simply less interested in the talk topics, and thus likely to score lower on exam questions anyway.[20]

This nuanced interpretation introduced by conscientious, replication-minded scientists stands as a stark contrast to how popular culture has latched onto the idea that laptops hurt learning. It's especially notable how so many people ascribe inherent power to the act of writing by hand.

Handwriting is dramatically different than keyboarding in many ways, I will grant you that. However, as a cognitive scientist with a deep background in the psychology of language, I can also assure you that writing with a handheld instrument has no special power as far as memory is concerned. There's no superhighway to long-term storage opened up by slowly scratching out words on paper, although you might think there was based on the breathless pronouncements in popular press about its power to sear information into your brain.[21]

This leads us back to a pretty inescapable conclusion about note-taking methodologies and machinery: It's the thought processes, not the medium itself, that matters most. Good note taking is a skill, one that can be consciously applied even when you have the option to do the kinds of mindless copying that is admittedly easier when on a laptop.

Imagine if even a tiny fraction of the energy directed against in-class laptops were directed toward promoting better ways to make the most of class time. Instructors could work on developing powerful methods for note taking, ones grounded in science and designed to maximize both the encoding and storage functions of notes. We could spend class time actually teaching those methods to students, and we could work to ensure that students get practice and feedback while they're developing this bedrock academic skill. That, to me, would be a crusade worth getting behind, and I have a hunch that it's something the Mueller, Morehead, Urry, and other research teams would all agree on.

They agree on something else as well, a limitation of their research that rarely makes it into any of the public discussions but which is spelled out quite clearly in several of the key articles on the subject. This is the issue of using laptops for off-topic, distracting activities in the middle of a learning task. In the actual studies, this wasn't possible, given that in the Mueller and Oppenheimer study as well as in the major replications, research participants were prevented from web surfing during the procedure.

Off-task activities made possible by laptops may not have been a major concern for these particular research teams, but they are for those of us teaching in real classrooms. Any faculty member who's ever watched a student gazing intently at a screen, nary a keystroke in sight, for an entire class period knows that note-taking technique isn't the issue, but instead whether the student is mentally present at all. At that point, the finer distinctions of encoding, storage, word count and verbatim overlap go out the window, and we're back to the fact that without attention, nothing much is going to happen as far as memory for class material is concerned.

This frustrating fact could be what really forms the reactor core powering the nuclear-level outrage about laptop-toting college students: that the devices enable them to tune in intermittently at best, ignoring their instructor the rest of the time. These instructors, being only human and having human egos, end up feeling personally slighted, or outright insulted. This is natural, but we should acknowledge that if this is the real motivation, the concern doesn't actually have much to do with the cognitive benefits of handwritten notes, or even with learning per se.

That said, it is a problem to have something as distracting as a computer in front of you when you're being asked to engage in the difficult and sometimes draining work of learning. Or even worse, if you are a student who is putting in the effort to stay focused in class, you may find yourself sucked in to the digital mayhem unfolding on your less conscientious neighbors' laptops.

This possibility was the subject of another high-profile study on distractions and laptops, carried out by the psychologists Faria Sana, Tina Weston, and Nicholas Cepeda.[22] They used a straightforward procedure to look at what other people's visible laptops do to performance, assigning volunteers to take handwritten notes during a lecture. One randomly assigned group was seated in view of research confederates who were flipping back and forth among different non–class-related websites, such as Facebook; others were only in view of other students taking handwritten notes. Those who could see others doing distracting things on laptops performed worse on a test of lecture content, validating the concern that it's not just one's own learning that suffers when laptops are misused in class.

Another problem that's rarely discussed, but which is equally important, is the distancing effect that laptops can have in a face-to-face class setting. Especially in seminar-style courses where students are supposed to be fully engaged with each other in deep discussion, those ever-present screens form a psychological and physical barrier. And although it's clear that good note-taking skills should offset the "mindless transcription" that laptop note-taking studies talk about, not all students have those skills, and not all instructors are willing and able to teach them.

This is a real problem. So what should instructors do?

The often-prescribed advice to forbid all laptops from all classrooms isn't a good option; here is why: access, inclusion, and simple consideration of individual needs. Some students need to be able to boost their writing speed, and to capture more of what's being said. Some need the additional structure provided by having an outline or a copy of the lecture slides that they can use as a guide as they go.

Some students are physically less capable of producing

legible, reasonably complete notes when handwriting. This point is personal. I have struggled tremendously with handwriting since I was in elementary school, partly because of a childhood injury that affected fine motor control in my dominant hand. Writing, for me, is slow, uncomfortable, and—given how illegible even my better attempts are—singularly unrewarding. These problems have only gotten worse with age (and, admittedly, with the lack of practice wrought by my own preference not to handwrite except when I absolutely have to). Given all of this, I'm the last person who would tell a student that in my class that it's paper notes or the highway.

Clearly, across-the-board, no-tech-allowed policies aren't the answer, especially if they are punitive or create a situation where individual accommodations are obvious to others. As an alternative, some instructors—myself included, at least in some classes—explicitly tell students that they can use any technology in any way they want during class, as long as it helps them learn and doesn't get in the way of others' learning. Knowing that it's easy to kid ourselves about what actually is helping our learning, I also like to encourage students to educate themselves about attention and learning, and to be really honest with themselves about how they are using technology. Once again, I borrow the lessons from *Attention Matters!*, and attempt to raise awareness about the fact that even if you're young and tech-savvy, your attention is more fallible than you realize and learning can't happen if you don't have your head in the game.

Other advocates go further, telling us to turn the spotlight onto our own teaching rather than on our students' failure to pay rapt attention to our every word. As teaching expert Robert Talbert put it in an insightful blog post about fighting in-class distraction:

"I think all lecturers, even the 1%-ers who are consistently out-standing lecturers, struggle to win the battle for attention. But, when you reach this point—which you will, if you teach for any length of time—you cannot just question the *technology*. You also need to question your *teaching*. By simply banning laptops when you get to this point, you're saying: *Everything I am doing is OK. It's that darn technology that's messing it up*. . . . So maybe the answer here isn't to ban laptops but to back away from instructional methods that are obviously going to invite distraction, and instead do class differently with the above questions in mind. We can even conceive of such classes where technology is *part* of the engagement process if we just try a little."[23]

These days, lecturing excessively—or lecturing at all, according to some experts—is generally seen as poor pedagogy. I come down in the middle on the issue of how much lecture is acceptable in a college class. On the one hand, a well-structured lecture can pack in lots of information in a compact form, and if the lecture content is well-connected to other learning activities that are going on in the class, that immediacy can trigger great retention of that material. I also think the enduring popularity of spoken-word media such as TED talks also demonstrates that good lectures can be engrossing, enjoyable, and have the power to truly move people.

On the other hand, I don't believe lecturing should be seen as synonymous with "teaching," nor should it be the default choice when we're planning what to do with class time. Even those carefully crafted, built-to-entertain TED talks are less than about 20 minutes long, much less than the typical class period. And as we saw back in the chapter on attention, it's natural for our engagement to wane—and distractions to beckon—if we're merely watching and taking in information for long stretches of time. There's also the practical reality that in college, our face-to-face meeting time is precious and limited, and in an era when there are so many ways to present and consume content, it doesn't make sense to spend that limited time simply restating information that students can get elsewhere.

Lecture may still be prevalent, but many faculty have incorporated this message about active learning into their teaching. And so, students are frequently encountering plenty of in-class activities that don't have anything to do with lecture, and where capturing material transmitted from the instructor isn't even relevant. Note taking during activities like pair discussion, laboratory exercises, role playing, quiz games and the like would be entirely beside the point. Students would be retaining memories of these exercises, all right, but more as an organic outcome of having had a compelling experience, not as something that happens through deliberately recording, condensing, and rehearsing information.

Talbert's point also implies that if we teachers are conceiving of class as an exercise in teacher-to-student information transfer (there's that banking metaphor again!), then no wonder students will treat it as such. Namely, they'll treat it as something to be mindlessly transcribed, and quite possibly, to be escaped from as often as possible. When we flip the script so that class is seen as something that students *do* instead of something that they witness and watch, suddenly the laptop question is less relevant.

Let's take the example of a class that kicks off with a fast-paced quiz game on the assigned background reading. The quiz then leads into an unscripted, lively discussion of what students got right and wrong. From there, the instructor introduces a structured discussion exercise in which groups of students each discuss one claim that was made in the reading they did, answering specific challenging questions without obvious right or wrong answers. At the end, each group presents their ideas to the rest of the class. The instructor summarizes the main points and adds a few additional questions for students to think about before the next meeting.

This, by the way, is a fair description of many of my own class meetings, complete with quizzes and structured exercises. Many students are in fact on various devices during class, to review the reading that's being discussed, search the Internet for additional evidence, definitions and the like, and perhaps even to take notes. Are they fooling around on them? Possibly, but given the fast pacing and the expectation that everyone will contribute to the tasks at hand, there's not too much opportunity for students to be pulled off course. And given that most of the time, the focus is supposed to be on them and not on me, occasional misuses of technology don't feel quite as much like an ego-bruising affront to me and my lecturing prowess.

Granted, this is an idealistic view of what class can be like, and it's one that is harder to pull off under less-privileged circumstances. Factors like large class sizes, lack of in-class teaching assistants, or less-prepared students do matter, enough where we shouldn't underestimate the challenge of creating active, engaged classrooms. But enough experts have weighed in on these kinds of teaching techniques by now to make it clear that active learning is both necessary and possible, even in the kind of courses that have traditionally fallen into the passive-learning, lecture-heavy model.[24] In other words, lecture does its job best when it's interspersed with other activities, and in my experience, pretty much any lecture-based course is improved by the introduction of these alternatives.

I also don't believe you need to have just one idealized kind of class—small, advanced, seminar-style, with perfectly motivated students—in order to buffer yourself from the problems of mobile devices. What you do need is an approach to teaching that makes every moment count, and at its best, entices students to set aside distractions voluntarily.

This brings us to one last perspective on in-class technology that I think is both practical, mindful of the science around distraction, and compassionate toward the needs of diverse learners. It's a philosophy that teaching expert and college professor James Lang articulates in the book *Distracted: Why Students Can't Focus and What You Can Do About It,*[25] which I also talked about in the previous chapter.

As you'd assume from the title, the book takes an in-depth look at the classroom problems wrought by mobile tech. As for the question of whether instructors ought to allow laptops, Lang offers a nuanced "it depends."

Instructors should make policies about technology, Lang says, but these should be responsive, situational, and part of a larger emphasis on purposeful use of every moment of class time. They should also be designed with an eye to the fact that devices don't just distract the person using them, as we've discussed in this chapter as well. Lang also reminds us that today's applications have been extraordinarily well engineered to seize our attention. In that sense, it's asking too much to expect students to resist through willpower alone.

This context-specific approach means that if there is a lecture, laptops are okay. If students are taking notes, it really doesn't matter how they choose to do it. But if there is a discussion, devices should be put away most or all of the time. The same goes for exercises, problem solving, and the like. In other words, if there's no clear and compelling reason why students should be writing, devices go away.

These are all specific directives without much in the way of loopholes, hedging or exceptions. However, it is possible to present the rules to students respectfully and with transparency about the reasoning behind them. I also like the fact that they don't flow out of the idea that technology is bad because all eyes and brains should be on the instructor at every moment. Instead, the policies seem to me to offer respect to the fact that attention is effortful. Staying focused when we are trying to learn is plain *hard*. This applies not just to the technology-dependent students of today, but for everyone, probably going back to the dawn of education itself.

It follows from this that, as Lang puts it, "if we wish to achieve attention in the classroom, we must cultivate it deliberately. The achievement of student attention requires deliberate and conscious effort from the teacher. We won't get students' attention by scolding them, at least in the long term. We won't get it from simply hoping for the best. We won't get it from going about our business in the front of the room and letting them fend for themselves out there in the seats. We'll get attention when we establish it as an important value in our courses and consider how we will help students cultivate and sustain the forms of attention that help them learn."[26]

Lang's formula isn't easy, nor is it simple. But it respects the common struggle at the heart of all focused learning, and offers a positive pathway forward, through leadership that is strong but also compassionate.

I want to end this chapter with a confession: I am still working on my own policies about mobile technology in classes, and I'm not totally happy with any of the ones I've tried. Lately I've leaned toward the laissez-faire side of the spectrum, out of a mix of concern about access, an aversion to constantly playing the role of enforcer, and an infusion of my own personal baggage surrounding the whole topic of writing by hand. But then again, when I've taught larger classes in the past, with assistants who could help with surveillance and so on, I've also had a stricter policy about when and how laptops could be used. I'd like to try Lang's method next time I've got this sort of class, where there are definite boundaries around different activities and a risk that students could be disrupting one another's focus.

In a way, my struggles reflect the larger state of affairs in the field of education, where—as I mentioned at the top of this chapter—we're still not quite sure where mobile devices fit into our mission and agenda. Many of us see the potential contained in the world-changing invention of computers that can and do go everywhere. But we in education also see the problems—literally, in the rows of laptop lids and smartphone screens that get between us and our students.

And so, as polarizing as the mobile-technology debates have been, I hope we keep having them. They are what will help us in education move beyond quiz games and the occasional in-class research assignment to turn the extraordinary power of mobile devices to our own purposes: accelerating learning and creating avenues to learning for more people throughout the world.

Can we have it both ways, using mobile technology to do great things while avoiding the side effects, risks, and aggravations that come with it? Maybe not entirely. Until such time as the devices are fundamentally redesigned—to neutralize notifications, to encourage judicious use rather than dispensing constant quick hits of information and entertainment—they're going to tilt toward eroding, not supporting, deep learning.

CHAPTER SUMMARY

- Concerns about technology have been heightened and concentrated by advances in mobile computing. Smartphones in particular represent a new level of influence on cognitive processes, given that they are designed to go everywhere and be a part of nearly every aspect of life.

- Research has offered a mixed set of findings on deeper cognitive and neural impacts of smartphones. It is unlikely that these devices have changed cognition in major ways, but relying on phone-based searches, in particular, may have subtle effects on memory and on the ability to engage in focused, demanding problem solving.

- The research on attention and smartphones is more clear-cut. Notifications disrupt attention even when they're not responded to right away, and merely having a cell phone in view might be distracting, even when it's not in use.

- Smartphones are frequently used to supplement memory through photos and also by GPS-aided navigation. Both of these uses can block the formation of new memories, making it so that we remember less about experiences and are less likely to develop good mental maps of locations we've visited.

- Mobile devices can also make positive contributions to learning, such as when they're used to engage students in retrieval practice. Examples include mobile-based quizzing and language learning applications.

- The debate over laptop-based versus handwritten note taking has generated intense attention, but the research support in favor of handwriting is frequently overstated. Multiple replication studies have demonstrated that the kind of verbatim transcription people tend to do on laptops is associated with lower exam performance; however, there is no consistent overall advantage for handwritten notes.

TEACHING TAKE-AWAYS

- Encourage students to get out of the habit of always searching for information using their smartphones. Although the evidence isn't definitive, there's some suggestion that over-reliance on search weakens their own memory for what they're looking up, and may also weaken some aspects of their thinking skills.
- If you take students on field trips or other similar in-the-field experiences, address how you expect phones to be used, or not used, during that time. Especially if students might be using their phones to take photos, advise them on how to do so in ways that are less likely to detract from memory—or alternatively, forbid picture taking altogether.
- Consider discussing with students the uniquely distracting nature of smartphones. Putting these devices out of sight during any demanding activity, including class and homework sessions, makes sense.
- At the same time, stay abreast of mobile apps that can advance students' learning. For example, quizzing apps such as Kahoot! or Quizlet do a great job at supporting retrieval practice, polling applications such as Poll

Everywhere are good for gathering anonymous input, and there are other specialized apps such as language learning programs that might fit with your own discipline and goals.

- Set structured policies for in-class mobile devices, but don't do so on the basis of research purportedly showing that writing by hand is superior. Instead, focus on what you think students should be doing (listening, participating in discussion, completing assigned work) at different points in the flow of your class, and then consider how devices might add to or take away from those activities.

- If you do want students to remember more of what they write down in class, consider offering a short module or other guidance on note-taking techniques. Regardless of the specific technique you choose, ensure that it encourages students to synthesize and paraphrase, rather than transcribe, what they're hearing in class.

—

HOW MEMORY CAN THRIVE IN A TECHNOLOGY-SATURATED FUTURE

—

For those of us who are passionate about our own learning as well as other people's learning: What should we conclude about the ways in which memory is changing in the contemporary world?

Based on what is known right now about human memory—which is a lot—we can identify some clear paths forward. There are points that are relevant specifically to teachers, and other more general points that are relevant to everyone. There are also some predictions for how practices and experiences involving memory could continue to evolve along with our technologies. These forward-looking possibilities are what I want to share with you in this final chapter.

The first few take-home ideas are ones of reassurance and a bit of moderation. Based on the best research to date, we can rest assured that our memories are not being permanently and seriously damaged. Don't worry—your brain cells aren't shorting out each time you press the Unlock button or succumb to a bout of scrolling. Relying on your laptop's memory isn't wiping out your own.

However, we do need to keep tabs on the costs of technology reliance in our everyday lives. More than ever before in human history, we need to be fierce and vigilant protectors of our cognitive capabilities, especially those involving attention. We also need to be deliberate about constructing memory so that we save what we actually need to remember, in the course of our lives as 21st century human beings. This means making a deliberate effort to smoothing the path to memory for information that might not grab us in the moment, but which contributes to our long-term thriving. Memory can and does happen automatically, all the time. But to be able to make the most of it, to retain not just the attention-grabbing or shocking things but the substantive ones as well—that requires deliberate strategy and deliberate effort. By stepping outside the process, to reflect on how and why we remember, we can be more in charge and leave less to chance.

The best research currently available in the field also tells us that generational differences, while real (and still developing), don't really come down to technology per se. Technology preferences are widely diverse within as well as between generations, and young people are unlikely to be clamoring for more technology for its own sake as part of their educations. That said, the more subtle impacts of having so many of one's life experiences mediated by technology have already been set in motion. Today's children, adolescents, and young adults will be able to look back on their life stories completely differently than people ever have before, with those stories likely being both more accurate and also less personal as a function of being anchored in digital rather than human episodic memory.

Younger people entering college and professions will also

be doing so with a greater habitual reliance on technology than ever before. In some ways, for young people, memory *is* the technology used to reinforce it. Consider how a typical 20-year-old of today would react to the prospect of losing a phone, or worse, losing a whole cloud-based storage cache. It's a panic-inducing thought, perhaps even more so than how members of earlier generations would have felt about losing a planner or address book. It is also a sentiment echoed by over 80% of people in one survey, who agreed that losing their external, technology-based memories would be devastating.[1] This is because so much of the information contained in digital accounts is highly personal, highly visual, and intimately tied to identity and experience.

Growing up with technology might make younger people dependent on their technology, but this doesn't mean they can't be thoughtful and even critical consumers of it. My experiences with college students all point toward their insights, their concerns, and their creativity concerning ways to keep technology under control. Perhaps growing up with devices strewn everywhere has made them realize that trying to stuff the tech genie back in the bottle is neither realistic nor desirable. Or perhaps they've learned through hard experience the importance of owning your technology rather than letting it own you. Whatever the reasons, I think we can heartily endorse the idea that the next generation of technology users are more than capable of leadership in this arena, and I look forward to finding out what they, as a group, envision for the future role of technology in all of our lives.

Advice for Teachers

For people who teach—formally or informally—there are some clear takeaways as well.

Actively engage your students in the common challenges
we all face with distraction, technology, and memory.

Our research at Northern Arizona University illustrates just
how receptive students can be to talking about the challenges of living with technology, especially the challenges
that put learning at risk. Time and again, I've read students'
fiery, first-person accounts of how frustrated they've been
with the risks and downsides—everything from the heart-
stopping danger of texting in traffic to the annoyance of
sitting next to classmates who are misusing their devices in
class. I've read their clever and creative solutions, and seen
the insights gained after they've completed a few engaging,
nonjudgmental activities designed to kick off thoughtful
discussion.

Those points are key, though: nonjudgmental, and coming
from a place of *common* challenge—not an us-versus-them,
kids-these-days stance. It's also important to consider
"what's next" after the acknowledgment that distraction
impairs memory. Just knowing that the problem exists isn't
enough, and neither is wanting to do better. Giving students
the basic tools of intentional behavior change, as we tried
to do with the *Attention Matters!* project, is the last step to
putting them in control of their technology for the long haul.

It's also important to pair the negative (Don't use your
phone in class! No laptops allowed!) with positive strategies—in other words, emphasizing what you *do* want students to do at least as much as what you *don't* want them to
do. Much of applied memory research can be boiled down
into principles that, while sometimes counterintuitive, are
easy for anyone to put into action. Learning about the amazing power of retrieval practice, for example, or why spacing is
important, can vastly expand a student's ability to remember

more information in less study time. It also reminds them that they need to put in effort and also deliberately design their study regimens. Passivity is out, and active involvement is in—not because we teachers demand to have their eyes on us at all times, but because students want and need to get the most they can out of time invested. This is a message I've seen resonate hundreds of times as students take the lessons of memory and make them their own.

Don't be afraid to ask students to commit material to memory.

It is now well past time for the pendulum to swing back, if not all the way to 1940s-style rote memorization, toward an acceptance that memory is one foundational part of a student's education. Every discipline has its key, don't-stop-to-Google-it knowledge, and it's up to instructors to select and present that information to students in a way that makes it clear that students really do need to have it down cold in order to succeed.

Some smart marketing is also in order, and it's good to have a plan going in for how to sell students on the idea of memorization. Here is where generational differences might crop up again, especially among students who are more technology dependent. Even something like how to spell key terms might not be something they think is important to remember, a fact which will show up in some unanticipated ways as we open up the dialogue about memory.

It shouldn't be *that* hard a sell though, when you explain to students that (a) you have been selective and strategic about what you are asking them to memorize, and (b) when you also teach techniques that make doing so a whole lot easier. Students are also quite open to new ideas about memory when you illustrate for them, as transparently as possible, why having a solid knowledge base is going to benefit them in their future work lives.

As teachers, we also know that selective and strategic memorization helps accomplish another high-priority agenda item, which is developing students' ability to engage in sophisticated, expert-level thinking. The research literature is beginning to show a promising pattern by which learning more, and learning more efficiently (through retrieval practice, for example) supports and accelerates the ability to categorize, infer, and draw conclusions. This is relatively new work and will no doubt be expanded and discussed more as the story unfolds. But I think there's more than enough evidence right now to make teachers feel confident in a decision to push memory further to the foreground.

*Don't be afraid to bring technology into the classroom—
but don't feel like you have to, either.*

Many of today's standout technologies for learning are laser focused on memory and helping students build knowledge efficiently. Kahoot!, Duolingo, Quizlet—all of these now have a solid track record for being both easy to use and well aligned with the science of memory. They work well either in the context of instructor-designed, instructor-led activities, or in the context of students' using them when they're studying independently. There are also a few educational technology applications out there that are geared to specific topic areas [2]; perhaps future years will see more of these pop up as faculty experiment with ways to leverage the visual and multimedia capabilities of mobile devices for teaching tough concepts within their own disciplines.

These hot applications of today are surely going to be replaced, though, and so it's important to remember what to look for in future ed-tech products intended to strengthen and develop knowledge. The main one is the capability for encouraging active recall of key information—features like lots of questions that students can answer, or the ability for instructors (or students themselves) to easily input lots of questions that they make up. If applications are also fun to use, if they support friendly competition, or open up other ways to make learning social—so much the better.

Teachers should also keep in mind that not all students, regardless of age, are going to want to use technology as part of their education. Unless it's critical that students do so in order to reach the learning objectives of the course, teachers should also be developing their own slate of low-tech alternatives. In-class polling, where students answer questions in real time, works brilliantly on phones and laptops, but something similar can be accomplished through asking students to hold up color-coded pieces of paper or turn in handwritten answers on index cards. Students who don't want to participate in something like a live Kahoot! quiz can still benefit by watching the display and noting down answers on paper as they go.

Forbid personal technology in class if you must,
but think carefully before you do.

No doubt there are times when personal technology is superfluous to an in-class learning activity, and plenty of times when it can get in the way. But the across-the-board tech ban should not be the default response. Students need and deserve some latitude to take notes in the ways that work best for them, and not to have those choices end up exposing any limitations or special needs that they would prefer to keep private. Bans don't always work in the classroom, and they definitely don't work when students are on their own learning at home, as in a fully online class.

And as we've seen throughout this book, the research that's frequently touted as offering reasons for limiting or flat-out rejecting technology is too often over-interpreted. Even good-quality studies don't always replicate, and the cautions that the researchers themselves put on the results—important limitations on concluding cause and effect or how well the effects would generalize to realistic situations—too frequently get lost in a rush to conclude that technology is damaging, and that science proves it so.

Advice for Everyone

Broadening our perspective beyond classrooms, what else should all of us as technology-using humans take away that will help us thrive?

Be protective about attention and vigilant against anything that detracts from it.

Distraction is kryptonite for memory, and unfortunately, distraction is what personal technology does best. Left unchecked, the alerts generated by the myriad programs that most of us use in the course of a day will inevitably erode memory. This is not because the constant interruptions permanently alter us at a fundamental level, but because they interfere with the process of making new memories when they're happening. This is a significant threat.

Guarding against such threats requires foresight and a fair amount of willpower. And so, just as teachers should include a dose of "how" along with the "what" of managing distraction, everyone else should familiarize themselves with some psychology-based tools for following through on intentions. Precommitment is one that's particularly well suited to the challenge. Site-blocking technology is a great way to help us ensure that our future selves behave the way that our present selves want them to, by delineating in advance exactly what you are and are not allowed to do at a given time. These limitations protect our limited stores of willpower against the depletion wrought by watching alert after alert pile up, and help insulate us from the constant pull of email and news. The do-not-disturb and call blocking functions now built into smartphone operating systems can similarly excuse us from responding to every single bid for our attention. They can also be configured to allow through the most important and relevant alerts, such as phone calls from family members or Slack messages from our current top-priority project group.

These are all concrete, attainable steps we can take to better manage our technology, without throwing it out. Even so, I sometimes get pushback from people who point out that, for example, using an application called SelfControl to block sites is the opposite of "self" control. We ought to be able to manage without needing those guardrails in place, and if we can't—well, then we shouldn't have the technology at all.

Here's what I think about that line of criticism. It's true that we've always had temptations that pull us away from our priorities—television, games, the water cooler at work, you name it. But for the first time ever, highly engineered versions of these activities are now accessible 24/7/365, and importantly, are available right within the spaces where many of us are now doing work—our phones, laptops, and tablets. And so, I think we need to take a cue from what the intentional behavior change experts have been saying for years and find ways to make it easier on ourselves to follow through on our plans, especially plans that help us stay the course when we're bored, overwhelmed, or otherwise predisposed to give in to temptation.

Use technology to buffer against prospective memory failures.

Although we should definitely minimize extraneous alerts that originate from other people, we should make liberal use of alerts that we ourselves set up. Tracking time and place is something that personal technology does incredibly well. In that way, it can help us advance our own priorities and avert disaster in the form of forgotten events and needed errands. Given that the human brain is typically terrible at this, it is a great thing to offload to technology.

Take and review digital photos strategically and with an eye to strengthening important episodic memories.

Used in the right ways, photos can be an incredibly effective way to spark recollection and strengthen memories of our life experiences. But let's also remember that used in the wrong way, digital photography can keep these great personal memories from forming in the first place. Probably the commonest of these wrong ways is in the attempt to capture too much of an experience in the moment, to the point where we're not engaged in the experience itself. Taking only a few pictures, or perhaps forgoing the camera altogether, is another deliberate strategy we can use to manage the risks. These risks are real; after all, no computer in the world can maintain real first-person episodic memories for you. Only you can do that, and in order to hang onto these memories you have to form them in the first place.

Don't assume that information will always be a click away.

As we share more and more of our factual memories with computers, the boundary between what we know and what they know may become even more porous. Knowing how and where to search out information is indeed an important contemporary skill, and does relieve us of the burden of having to memorize a lot of day-to-day minutiae.

However, researchers now know that our memories can subtly substitute the "where" for the "what" in memorized knowledge. And so, when we catch ourselves in the act of assuming that some important piece of information will always be an online search away, we can try to head that process off. For the more important things that we do want to have as part of our own stored knowledge, we should try to act as though we'll never be able to find it online, even when we probably could.

Be a skeptical, selective, and inquisitive consumer of research on technology and the mind.

We've seen how advice aimed at teachers frequently overstates and oversimplifies the impact of things like laptops on learning, and the same distortions happen in the more general sphere of reporting about technology's impacts. If a study you're reading about sounds so dramatically alarming that you want to drop your phone in the nearest recycling bin and go shopping for a vintage typewriter—that's a big red flag. Studies like this are often overreported or stretched to the breaking point. They're almost always in need of rigorous replication, or at the very least, much more nuanced summary. Every now and again, the wilder claims—like those involving the infamous "goldfish" study—turn out to be flat-out pseudoscience.

On the flip side, technology-as-brain-panacea messages are just as suspect. Here too, we've seen this dynamic play out in education, with the rise and fall of the idea that technology will fix every problem there is in learning, for all learners, by its mere presence.

In sum: It takes a lot to significantly and permanently alter the way the mind works, whether for good or bad. Research that seems to state otherwise deserves heavy scrutiny.

What the Future Holds

There's little doubt that new technologies will keep arriving on the scene, each with their own set of impacts on how we take in and remember information. One clear example that's especially hot today is virtual reality (VR), along with its cousin augmented reality (i.e., media that superimposes virtual sights, sounds, or other information onto a real-world scene). Educators have taken the idea of VR and run with it; at the time of this writing there are dozens of projects going on around the country seeking to create educational applications that get at learning in brand-new ways.

Time is going to tell how well these projects work out. The best information we have right now suggests that similar to other educational technologies, the effectiveness of educational VR depends on how well its unique characteristics match up with the material and the goals of the learning exercise. For example, VR programs that teach anatomy and physiology fit well with VR's 3-D visualization capabilities.[3] Similar to this idea, we've found in our own research at Northern Arizona University that VR can help teach organic chemistry, another subject where being able to interact with and view shapes from multiple perspectives is critically important.[4] As more educational VR applications become available, more instructors will be asking how—or whether—such programs enhance retention for the concepts students are supposed to be learning. And as more of us experience virtual reality in its many forms, we'll start to see how we remember differently when we're in one of these simulated environments.

Increases in the amount of media and cloud storage available to us will increase the importance of visual media for memory in the modern world. Just in the last ten years or so, we've gone from being able to share the occasional image on social media or shared database, to being able to store and swap as many as we could possibly want. TikTok, and before it the now-defunct Vine, have turned video from a specialized, capacity-eating medium to one that anyone can use just for fun. We'll likely see more of these "recreational" platforms come and go, but video as part of communication, commemoration, and sharing is here to stay.

Current trends also point to more people asking how their personal technology can best serve them, rather than just how much more the technology can do. The ability of a technology to serve up push notifications has now thoroughly lost any novelty value it once had with consumers, and more consumers may be looking for technology that does less, but does it better. Public discussion about technology and the mind may not have always been faithful to the research literature. But one great outcome is that it's spurred more people to question the role of personal tech in their lives, and encouraged more people to set deliberate parameters around when they use technology and how.

There's an additional development that I'll admit is more

a personal hope than an actual trend: I wonder whether we will see more people approaching memory not with dread but as a source of fun. Will we see a renaissance in the pleasure of remembering for its own sake? Will spelling bees, trivia contests, even memory competitions become more popular? As with so many other pursuits in modern life, memory is not a life-or-death necessity any more. And so, like cooking, crafting, hiking, or gardening—maybe memory will become something we do for fun, rather than solely something we have to do to survive.

This brings me to one last thing I want to share with you, a treasured memory of my own.

Whan that aprill with his shoures soote
The droghte of march hath perced to the roote,
And bathed every veyne in swich licour,
Of which vertu engendred is the flour;
Whan zephirus eek with his sweete breeth
Inspired hath in every holt and heeth
Tendre croppes, and the yonge sonne
Hath in the Ram his halve cours yronne,
And smale foweles maken melodye,
That slepen al the night with open ye . . .

These are the opening lines of the Prologue to Chaucer's *Canterbury Tales*, and there was a point at which I could rattle off each and every one by heart. This was thanks to my high school English teacher, Lynne Murchison, who was famous for her exacting standards and a level of innovative thinking not much seen in teaching back then. "Dr. Murk" required every student in her British Literature class to memorize the Prologue, bestowing a passing grade only when you could stand in front of her sans notes and say all the lines perfectly, in the original Middle English.

We students each set our own time to step up and take the challenge, one by one. If we messed up, we came back and we did it again, until we got it right. Each of us experimented with different ways to get the task done, with the ones who'd succeeded passing tips to those who were still working on it. Most commonly, what we hit upon in the course of this project was that we couldn't just take it word by unfamiliar and strange word. We had to try to understand the whole passage, to picture the scene that Chaucer was describing, and we had to try to think about why he wanted to describe it exactly as he did.

When Dr. Murchison died in 2020, her students shared the sad news online, as we all do these days. And right away, we started swapping stories about this one thing we did in class. How maddening but also how fun it was, and how exhilarating it was when we finally got the whole thing right. Some of her alums even say that they still know the lines to this day.

Her signature assignment may have seemed a bit eccentric even decades ago, and today this kind of academic requirement is even less common than it was back then. I would like to see this change. I'd like to see students—and everyone, actually—engage in this kind of memory challenge, and memory play, more often than we do.

I say this because the exercise, tough as it was, crushed no one's creativity, nor did it block us from going on to lives enriched by intellectual curiosity. It became a point of pride. And it taught all of us, without our realizing it at the time, techniques that we could use later on as we went on to professions and pursuits that required us to know our stuff.

Students *want* that sense of accomplishment. They want to have a sense of mastery connected to things they care about, even in an age that's defined by infinite capacity for digital memory.

Our human memories are quirky, limited, and no match for what even the most basic technology can do. But our memories will survive this technology, and paired with it in the right way, I know that they can thrive like they never have before.

NOTES

NOTES TO CHAPTER 1

1. G. Small & G. Vorgan (2008), Meet your iBrain, *Scientific American Mind, 19,* 42–49.
2. D. Norman (1993), *Things that make us smart: Defending human attributes in the age of the machine* (p. 43), Diversion Books.
3. G. Tracy (2019, May 5), How technology helps our memories, *The Week,* https://theweek.com/articles/836109/how -technology-helps-memories.
4. Parent quoted in N. Bowles (2018, October 26), A dark consensus about screens and kids begins to emerge in Silicon Valley, *New York Times,* https://www.nytimes.com/2018/10/26 /style/phones-children-silicon-valley.html.
5. J. Anderson & L. Rainie (2018, April 17), *The future of well-being in a tech-saturated world.* Pew Research Center. https:// www.pewresearch.org/internet/2018/04/17/the-future-of-well -being-in-a-tech-saturated-world/.
6. S. Pinker (2010, June 10), Mind over mass media, *New York Times.*
7. J. Wilkins (1997), Protecting our children from Internet smut: Moral duty or moral panic? *The Humanist, 57,* 4. See also: R. J. Noonan (1998), The psychology of sex: A mirror from the Internet. In J. Gackenbach (Ed.), *Psychology and the Internet: Intrapersonal, interpersonal, and transpersonal implications* (pp 143–168), Academic Press.
8.   B. Auxier, M. Anderson, A. Perrin, & E. Turner (2020, July 28), *Parenting children in the age of screens,* https://www.pewresearch .org/internet/2020/07/28/parenting-children-in-the-age-of -screens/.
9. A. K. Przybylski & N. Weinstein (2017), Digital screen time

limits and young children's psychological well-being: Evidence from a population-based study, *Child Development*, *90*(1), e56-e65. https://doi.org/10.1111/cdev.13007.

10. See, for example, the Freewrite product: https://getfreewrite.com/.

11. R. Contreras (2017, June 15), Digital burnout leads to a resurgence of vintage typewriters, and it isn't just a fad, *Christian Science Monitor*. https://www.csmonitor.com/USA/Society/2017/0615/Digital-burnout-leads-to-a-resurgence-of-vintage-typewriters-and-it-isn-t-just-a-fad.

12. I can offer a personal testimonial that the site blocking capabilities of SelfControl are indeed impossible to evade through any normal means. https://selfcontrolapp.com/.

13. A. L. Duckworth, K. L. Milkman, & D. Laibson (2018), Beyond willpower: strategies for reducing failures of self-control, *Psychological Science in the Public Interest*, 19(3), 102–129, https://doi.org/10.1177/1529100618821893.

14. M. D. Miller (2014), *Minds Online: Teaching Effectively with Technology*, Harvard University Press.

15. E. Ellerman (1998), The internet in context. In Gackenbach, J. (Ed.), *Psychology and the Internet: Intrapersonal, interpersonal, and transpersonal implications* (pp 11–33), Academic Press.

16. G. Salomon & D. Perkins (2013), Do technologies make us smarter? Intellectual amplification *with, of,* and *through* technology, *in* R. Sternberg & D. Preiss (Eds), *Intelligence and technology: Ihe impact of tools on the nature and development of human abilities* (pp.71–86), Routledge. https://doi.org/10.4324/9780203824252.

17. See also D. Preiss & R. Sternberg (2013), Technologies for working intelligence, *in* R. Sternberg & D. Preiss (Eds), *Intelligence and technology: The impact of tools on the nature and development of human abilities* (pp. 87–101), Routledge, https://doi.org/10.4324/9780203824252.

18. D. Preiss & R. Sternberg (2013), Technologies for working intelligence, *in* R. Sternberg & D. Preiss (Eds), *Intelligence and technology: The impact of tools on the nature and development of human abilities* (pp. 87–101), New York: Routledge, https://doi.org/10.4324/9780203824252.

19. R. Nickerson (2013), Technology and cognitive amplification, *in* R. Sternberg & D. Preiss (Eds), *Intelligence and technology: The impact of tools on the nature and development of human abilities* (pp. 3–27), New York: Routledge, https://doi.org/10.4324/9780203824252.

20. R. Nickerson (2013), Technology and cognitive amplification, *in*

R. Sternberg & D. Preiss (Eds), *Intelligence and Technology: The impact of tools on the nature and development of human abilities* (pp. 3–27), New York: Routledge, https://doi.org/10.4324/9780203824252.

21. D. Norman (2013), *The design of everyday things* (Revised and expanded edition, p. 286), Basic Books.

22. See, for example, D. T. Willingham (2010, Summer), Have technology and multitasking rewired how students learn?, *American Educator*, 23–29; D. T. Willingham (2015, January 20), Smartphones don' t make us dumb, *New York Times*; S. Pinker (2010, June 10), Mind over mass media, *New York Times*.

23. S. Pinker (2010, June 10), Mind over mass media, *New York Times*.

24. G. W. Small, T. D. Moody, P. Siddarth, P., & S. Y. Bookheimer (2009), Your brain on Google: Patterns of cerebral activation during Internet searching, *American Journal of Geriatric Psychiatry*, 17(2), 116–126, https://doi.org/10.1097/JGP.0b013e3181953a02.

25. Keep in mind that fMRIs measure neural activity indirectly, usually by comparing the amount of blood flow to regions of the brain during a task of interest (in this case, searching) versus a control task of some kind. The control is subtracted from the task of interest, and the remaining activation is depicted by superimposing it on a representation of the brain, so that you end up with a picture that looks like "hot spots" or certain regions lighting up during the task of interest. In studies with more than one participant, data from multiple people are also averaged or combined to make up these composite images. Researchers also statistically analyze these increases or decreases in regional blood flow in response to the change in tasks, to assess whether they are statistically significant.

26. This additional part about experience was reported in a different publication by the lead author: G. Small & G. Vorgan (2008), Meet your iBrain, *Scientific American Mind*, 19, 42–49.

27. The sample-size issue is a generic criticism that's almost guaranteed to come up in coverage of the limitations of this study, or really of any study of its kind. It's frequently conflated with the *representativeness* of the sample, which is a separate issue and one that is not addressed by simply adding more people to the study. Appropriate sample size is something that can be determined using conventional guidelines and calculation methods, but there isn't one gold-standard minimum number that applies across the board. In sum:

Sample size is a more complicated question than meets the eye, and press coverage of sampling rarely gets it right.

28. G. Small & G. Vorgan (2008), Meet your iBrain, *Scientific American Mind*, *19*, 42–49.

29. See, for example, these classic articles on cognitive aging: D. G. MacKay & D. M. Burke (1990), Cognition and aging: a theory of new learning and the use of old connections, *Aging and Cognition: Knowledge Organization and Utilization*, 213–263, https://doi.org/10.1016/S0166-4115(08)60159-4; L. Hasher & R. T. Zacks (1988), Working memory, comprehension, and aging: A review and a new view, *Psychology of Learning and Motivation—Advances in Research and Theory*, *22*(C), 193–225, https://doi.org/10.1016/S0079-7421(08)60041-9.

30. G. W. Small, T. D. Moody, P. Siddarth, P., & S. Y. Bookheimer (2009), Your brain on Google: patterns of cerebral activation during internet searching. *American Journal of Geriatric Psychiatry*, *17*(2), 116–126. https://doi.org/10.1097/JGP .0b013e3181953a02, p. 116.

31. Here's one example: J. Harris (2010, August 20), How the internet is altering your mind, *The Guardian*. Retrieved from https://www.theguardian.com/technology/2010/aug/20 /internet-altering-your-mind

32. UCLA Health (2008, October 14), *UCLA study finds that searching the Internet increases brain function*, https://www .uclahealth.org/ucla-study-finds-that-searching-the-internet -increases-brain-function.

33. J. Feifer (2014, October 13), *The Internet is not harming you. Here's what's harmful: Fearmongering about the Internet*, Fast Company, https://www.fastcompany.com/3036428/fear-and -loathing-of-silicon-valley?cid=search.

34. This book offers an excellent account of the deep changes wrought by literacy: M. Wolf (2007), *Proust and the squid: The story and science of the reading brain*, HarperCollins.

35. J. Feifer (2014, October 13), *The Internet is not harming you. Here's what's harmful: Fearmongering about the Internet*, Fast Company, https://www.fastcompany.com/3036428/fear -and-loathing-of-silicon-valley?cid=search.

36. S. Pinker (n.d.), *How is the internet changing the way you think?* Edge, https://www.edge.org/responses/how-is-the-internet -changing-the-way-you-think.

37. T. Tokuhama-Espinosa (2018), *Neuromyths: Debunking false ideas about the brain*, New W.W. Norton.

38. R. Nickerson (2013), Technology and cognitive amplification, in R. Sternberg & D. Preiss (Eds), *Intelligence and technology: The*

impact of tools on the nature and development of human
abilities (pp. 3–27), Routledge, https://doi.org/10.4324
/9780203824252, quote on p. 25.

NOTES TO CHAPTER 2

1. Which I wouldn't dream of repeating in a high-toned book such
   as this one.
2. Benedict Cumberbatch.
3. D. J. Simons & C. F. Chabris (2011), What people believe
   about how memory works: A representative survey of the U.S.
   population, *PLoS ONE*, *6*(8), https://doi.org/10.1371/journal
   .pone.0022757.
4. K. Betts, M. Miller, T. Tokuhama-Espinosa, P. Shewokis,
   A. Anderson, C. Borja, T. Galoyan, B. Delaney, J. Eigenauer,
   & S. Dekker (2019), International report: Neuromyths and
   evidence-based practices in higher education, Online Learning
   Consortium, Newburyport, MA.
5. A survey of the general population conducted through the
   online Amazon Mechanical Turk platform found that a similar
   percent—26%—agreed with the same question. J.R. Finley,
   F. Naaz, & F.W. Goh (2018), Memory and technology: How we
   use information in the brain and in the world. Springer.
6. D. J. Simons & C. F. Chabris (2011), What people believe
   about how memory works: A representative survey of the U.S.
   population, *PloS ONE*, *6*(8), https://doi.org/10.1371/journal
   .pone.0022757, p. 7.
7. E. Loftus, & J. Palmer (1974), Reconstruction of automobile
   destruction: An example of the interaction between language
   and memory, *Journal of Verbal Learning and Verbal Behavior*, *13*
   (5), 585–589.
8. J. F. Kihlstrom (1997), Hypnosis, memory and amnesia,
   *Philosophical Transactions of the Royal Society B: Biological
   Sciences*, *352*(1362), 1727–1732, https://doi.org/10.1098
   /rstb.1997.0155.
9. D. J. Simons & C. F. Chabris (2011), What people believe
   about how memory works: A representative survey of the U.S.
   population, *PloS ONE*, *6*(8), https://doi.org/10.1371/journal
   .pone.0022757.
10. D. J. Simons & C. F. Chabris (1999), Gorillas in our midst:
    Sustained inattentional blindness for dynamic events,
    Perception, *28*(9), 1059–1074, https://doi.org/10.1068/p2952.
11. See also: M. D. Miller (2011), What college teachers should
    know about memory: A perspective from cognitive psychology,

College Teaching, 59, 117–122; G. Plancher & P. Barrouillet (2019), On some of the main criticisms of the modal model: Reappraisal from a TBRS perspective, *Memory and Cognition, 48*(3), 455–468. https://doi.org/10.3758/s13421-019 -00982-w.

12. R. Atkinson & R. M. Shiffrin (1971), The control of short-term memory, *Scientific American, 22,* 82–90.

13. R. C. Martin (1993), Short-term memory and sentence processing: Evidence from neuropsychology, *Memory & Cognition 21,* 176–83; R. C. Martin & S. D. Breedin (1992), Dissociations between speech perception and phonological short-term memory deficits, *Cognitive Neuropsychology, 9.* 509–534.

14. M. D. Miller (2011), What college teachers should know about memory: A perspective from cognitive psychology, *College Teaching, 59*(3), 117–122,https://doi.org/10.1080/87567555 .2011.580636.

15. M. C. Potter & L. Lombardi (1990), Regeneration in the short-term recall of sentences, *Journal of Memory and Language, 29,* 633–654.

16. P. Freire (2014), *Pedagogy of the oppressed: 30th anniversary edition,* Bloomsbury.

17. K. Bain (2004), *What the best college teachers do* (p. 30), Harvard University Press.

18. G. A. Miller (1956), The magical number seven, plus or minus two: Some limits on our capacity for processing information, *Psychological Review, 63*(2), 81–97, https://doi-org.libproxy .nau.edu/10.1037/h0043158; see also G. A. Miller (1994), The magical number two, plus or minus one: Some limits on our capacity for processing musical information, *Psychological Review, 101*(2), 343–352, https://doi.org/10.1177 /102986490200600205; and A. Baddeley (1994), The magical number seven: Still magic after all these years? *Psychological Review, 101*(2), 353–356, https://doi.org/10.1037/0033-295X .101.2.353.

19. N. Cowan (2010), The magical mystery four: How is working memory capacity limited, and why? *Current Directions in Psychological Science, 19*(1), 51–57, https://doi.org/10.1177 /0963721409359277.

20. G. A. Miller (1956), The magical number seven, plus or minus two: some limits on our capacity for processing information, *Psychological Review, 63*(2), 81–97, https://doi-org.libproxy.nau .edu/10.1037/h0043158.

21. M. D. Miller (2011), What college teachers should know about

memory: A perspective from cognitive psychology, *College Teaching, 59*, 117–122.

22. J. L. Doumont (2002), Magical numbers: The seven-plus-or-minus-two myth, *IEEE Transactions on Professional Communication, 45*(2), 123–127, https://doi.org/10.1109/TPC.2002.1003695.

23. G. Plancher & P. Barrouillet (2019), On some of the main criticisms of the modal model: Reappraisal from a TBRS perspective, *Memory and Cognition, 48*(3), 455–468, https://doi.org/10.3758/s13421-019-00982-w.

24. A. D. Baddeley (1986), *Working memory,* Oxford University Press.

25. E. V. Chemerisova, & O. V. Martynova (2019), Effects of the phonological loop of working memory on the productivity of solving mathematical and verbal tasks in specialists in mathematics and the humanities, *Neuroscience and Behavioral Physiology, 49*(7), 857–862, https://doi.org/10.1007/s11055-019-00812-1.

26. R. C. Martin & T. T. Schnur (2019), Independent contributions of semantic and phonological working memory to spontaneous speech in acute stroke, *Cortex, 112*, 58–68, https://doi.org/10.1016/j.cortex.2018.11.017.

27. M. D. Miller (2011), What college teachers should know about memory: A perspective from cognitive psychology, *College Teaching, 59*, 117–122.

28. J. M. McQueen, F. Eisner, M. A. Burgering, & J. Vroomen (2019), Specialized memory systems for learning spoken words, *Journal of Experimental Psychology: Learning Memory and Cognition, 46*(1), 189–199, https://doi.org/10.1037/xlm0000704; M. L. Freedman & R. C. Martin (2001), Dissociable components of short-term memory and their relation to long-term learning, *Cognitive Neuropsychology*, https://doi.org/10.1080/02643290126002; A. Baddeley, S. Gathercole, & C. Papagno (1998), The phonological loop as a language learning device, *Psychological Review, 105*, 158–173.

29. This short article also has a description of how this process plays out in realistic learning situations: M. D. Miller (2012, September), Helping students memorize: Tips from cognitive science, *The Teaching Professor, 97*, 1–6.

30. See, for example: E. Tulving (2002), Episodic memory, *Annual Review of Psychology, 53*, 1–25. https://doi.org/10.1007/978-3-642-36172-2_201013; E. Tulving (1985), How many memory systems are there?, 385–398.

31. Sometimes this is also termed "declarative memory."

32. M. T. H. Chi & R. D. Koeske (1983), Network representation of a child's dinosaur knowledge, *Developmental Psychology, 19*(1), 29–39, https://doi.org/10.1037/0012-1649.19.1.29.

33. Technically speaking, tip-of-the-tongue states involve partial retrieval of a word; the abstract meaning is coming to mind, but the actual sounds are not. For a more fine-grained explanation of these errors, see this classic research article: D. M. Burke, D. MacKay, J. S. Worthley, & E. Wade (1991), On the tip of the tongue: What causes word finding failures in young and older adults?, *Journal of Memory and Language, 30*(5), 542–579, https://doi.org/10.1016/0749-596X(91)90026-G.

34. J. Ost, A. Vrij, A. Costall, & R. Bull (2002), Crashing memories and reality monitoring: Distinguishing between perceptions, imaginations and "false memories," *Applied Cognitive Psychology, 16*, 125–134.

35. K. Pezdek (2003), Event memory and autobiographical memory for the events of September 11, 2001, *Applied Cognitive Psychology, 17*(9), 1033–1045, https://doi.org/10.1002/acp.984.

36. W. Hirst, E. A. Phelps, R. L. Buckner, M. K. Johnson, K. B. Lyle, M. Mather, & K. J. Mitchell (2010), Long-term memory for the terrorist attack of September 11: Flashbulb memories, event memories, and the factors that influence their retention, *Journal of Experimental Psychology. General, 138*(2), 161–176, https://doi.org/10.1037/a0015527; K. Pezdek (2003), Event memory and autobiographical memory for the events of September 11, 2001, *Applied Cognitive Psychology, 17*(9), 1033–1045, https://doi.org/10.1002/acp.984.

37. D. R. Godden & A. D. Baddeley (1975), Context-dependent memory in two natural environments: On land and underwater, *British Journal of Psychology, 66*(3), 325–331, https://doi.org/10.1016/0195-6671(82)90042-8.

38. D. L. Schacter (1999), The seven sins of memory: Insights from psychology and cognitive neuroscience, *American Psychologist*, https://doi.org/10.1037/0003-066X.54.3.182; M. K. Johnson, S. Hashtroudi, & D. S. Lindsay (1993), Source monitoring, *Psychological Bulletin, 114*(1), 3–28, https://doi.org/10.1037/0033-2909.114.1.3.

39. D. T. Willingham (2008), Critical thinking: Why is it so hard to teach? *Arts Education Policy Review, 109*(4), 21–32, https://doi.org/10.3200/AEPR.109.4.21-32.

40. For an example and illustration, see https://www.purlsoho.com/create/long-tail-cast-on/

41. The cerebellum is the wrinkled roundish mass that looks almost

like a second miniature brain tacked onto the rear underside of the rest of the brain, just above the spinal cord.

42. S. Cavaco, S. W. Anderson, J. S. Allen, A. Castro-Caldas, & H. Damasio, H. (2004), The scope of preserved procedural memory in amnesia, *Brain, 127*(8), 1853–1867, https://doi .org/10.1093/brain/awh208.

43. F. I. Craik & R. S. Lockhart (1972), Levels of processing: A framework for memory research, *Journal of Verbal Learning and Verbal Behavior, 11,* 671–684.

44. Note that although depth of processing studies tend to involve fairly short delays—under an hour—between study and test phases, they're technically not tapping short-term memory. Short-term, immediate, or working memory, as memory researchers think of it, typically extends less than a minute—it's *really* short term.

45. T. B. Rogers, N.A. Kuiper, & W. S. Kirker (1977), Self-reference and the encoding of personal information, *Journal of Personality and Social Psychology, 35*(9), 677–688. https://doi.org/10.1037 /0022-3514.35.9.677.

46. E. J. Fantino, K. Fischer, D. Krebs, G. S. Reynolds, & Z. Rubin (1974), *Understanding Psychology*, CRM Books.

47. As an example, my total amnesia for the content of my freshman Western Civilization course probably reflects both of these factors. I never went on to use most of that information, contributing to its decay over time. I also lacked the conceptual understanding at the time that would allow me to interpret and organize what I was supposed to be learning. I was able to get by on the exams by memorizing a few facts, but I retained little that I could use over time.

48. For a variation on this idea, see J. S. Nairne (1990), A feature model of immediate memory, *Memory & Cognition, 18*(3), 251–269, https://doi.org/10.3758/BF03213879.

49. However, it's not impossible, as discussed in this story about the controversy over repressed memory: L. Winerman (2005), Can you force yourself to forget?, *Monitor on Psychology, 36*(8), 52, http://www.apa.org/monitor/sep05/forget.aspx.

50. S. Porter& K. A. Peace (2007), The scars of memory of traumatic and positive emotional memories in adulthood, *Psychological Science, 18*(5), 435–441, https://doi.org/10.1111 /j.1467-9280.2007.01918.x.

51. See, e.g., H. P. Bahrick (1984), Semantic memory content in permastore: Fifty years of memory for Spanish learned in school, *Journal of Experimental Psychology: General, 113,* 1–29

52. S. Porter & K. A. Peace (2007), The scars of memory of

traumatic and positive emotional memories in adulthood, *Psychological Science*, *18*(5), 435–441, https://doi.org/10.1111 /j.1467-9280.2007.01918.x.

53. See for example the discussion in this article: L. Fornazzari, M. Leggieri, T. A. Schweizer, R. L. Arizaga, R.F. Allegri, & C. E. Fischer (2018), Luria and Borges revisited, *Dementia & Neuropsychologia, 12* (2), 101-104, https://doi.org/10 .1590/1980-57642018dn12-020001.

54. An important caveat is that although S's memory was clearly extraordinary, it was not perfect nor complete in every way. For a recent discussion of some of the questions that still exist about the case of S, see R. Johnson (2017), The mystery of S., the man with an impossible memory, *The New Yorker*, 1–12.

55. The neuroscientist Luis Fornazzari and colleagues hypothesize that both hypermnesia and problems with executive functions could be the result of autism spectrum disorder: L. Fornazzari, M. Leggieri, T. A. Schweizer, R. L. Arizaga, R.F. Allegri, & C. E. Fischer (2018), Hyper memory, synaesthesia, savants: Luria and Borges revisited, *Dementia & Neuropsychologia, 12*(2), 101–104, https://doi.org/10.1590/1980-57642018dn12-020001.

56. W. James (1980: 689), *The Principles of Psychology*, Volume 1, New York: Henry Holt & Company, as cited in L. Fornazzari, M. Leggieri, T. A. Schweizer, R. L. Arizaga, R.F. Allegri, & C. E. Fischer (2018), Hyper memory, synaesthesia, savants: Luria and Borges revisited, *Dementia & Neuropsychologia, 12*(2), 101–104, https://doi.org/10.1590/1980-57642018dn12-020001.

NOTES TO CHAPTER 3

1. K. Robinson (2006, February), *Do schools kill creativity?* [Video], TED Conferences, https://www.ted.com/talks/sir_ken _robinson_do_schools_kill_creativity.

2. B. S. Bloom, M. Engelhart, E. J. Furst, W. Hill, & D. R. Krathwohl (1956), *Taxonomy of educational objectives, Handbook I: Cognitive domain*, Longman. For an updated version of this familiar "learning pyramid," see L. W. Anderson, & D. R. Krathwohl (Eds.) (2001), *A taxonomy for learning, teaching and assessing: A revision of Bloom's taxonomy of educational objectives: Complete edition*, Longman. For a recent illustration and explanation of Bloom's key concepts, see https://cft.vanderbilt .edu/guides-sub-pages/blooms-taxonomy/.

3. However, there are some alternative depictions that don't use the pyramid metaphor. For examples, see M. Knapp, (2016, October 11), 5 gorgeous depictions of Bloom's taxonomy,

https://news.nnlm.gov/nto/2016/10/11/5- gorgeous -depictions-of-blooms-taxonomy/.

4. For a similar take on the hierarchical nature of Bloom's taxonomy, see J. Lang (2016), *Small teaching: Everyday lessons from the science of learning*, Jossey-Bass.

5. D. Pogue (2013), Smartphones mean you will no longer have to memorize facts, *Scientific American*, 1–5, http://www .scientificamerican.com/article/smartphones-mean-no -longer-memorize-facts/.

6. L. G. Eglington & S. H. K. Kang (2018), Retrieval practice benefits deductive inference, *Educational Psychology Review*, *30*(1), 215–228. https://doi.org/10.1007/s10648-016 -9386-y.

7. J. D. Bransford & D. L. Schwartz (2001), Rethinking transfer: A simple proposal with multiple implications, *Review of Research in Education*, *2*, 61–100, https://aaalab.stanford.edu/papers /Rethinking_transfer_a_simple_proposal_with_multiple _implications.pdf.

8. See, for example, L. B. Nilson (2013), *Creating self-regulated learners: Strategies to strengthen students' self-awareness and learning skills*, Stylus; M. Saundra (2015), *Teach students how to learn: Strategies you can incorporate into any course to improve student metacognition, study skills, and motivation*, Stylus.

9. V. Sathy & K. A. Hogan (2019, July), Want to reach all of your students? Here's how to make your teaching more inclusive, *The Chronicle of Higher Education*, https://www.chronicle.com /interactives/20190719_inclusive_teaching.

10. I.e., "R can saw little rocks."

11. J. M. Lang (2011), Teaching and human memory, Part 2, *The Chronicle of Higher Education*.

12. D. T. Willingham (2017, May 19), You still need your brain, *New York Times*.

13. P. K. Agarwal (2019), Retrieval practice & Bloom's taxonomy: Do students need fact knowledge before higher order learning?, *Journal of Educational Psychology*, *111*(2), 189–209, https://doi .org/10.1037/edu0000282.

14. See, for example, C. Riener & D. Willingham (2010), The myth of learning styles, *Change: The Magazine of Higher Learning*, *42*(5), 32–35, https://doi.org/10.1080/00091383.2010.503139.

15. For a deep dive into the impact of emotions on learning, see S. R. Cavanagh (2016), *The spark of learning: Energizing the college classroom with the science of emotion*, West Virginia University Press.

16. P. W. Thorndyke (1977), Cognitive structures in comprehension

and memory of narrative discourse, *Cognitive Psychology*, *9*(1), 77–110, https://doi.org/10.1016/0010-0285(77)90005-6.

17. J. M. Lang (2019, January 4), How to teach a good first day of class. https://www.chronicle.com/article/how-to-teach-a -good-first-day-of-class/.

18. For an overview, see https://cft.vanderbilt.edu/guides-sub -pages/just-in-time-teaching-jitt/.

19. The definitive source for PBL resources geared to higher education is this site maintained by the University of Delaware: https://www.itue.udel.edu/resources/pbl-resources.

20. E. Sung & R. E. Mayer (2012), When graphics improve liking but not learning from online lessons, *Computers in Human Behavior*, *28*(5), 1618–1625, https://doi.org/10.1016/j.chb .2012.03.026.

21. This is also known as the "method of loci," and has been around for thousands of years as a way of memorizing lengthy sequences, such as the components of a speech.

22. For more on memorizing students' names, see this post I put up describing my own technique: https://www.academia .edu/38180533/Research_based_Tips_and_Tricks_for _Remembering_Names_pdf.

23. For some exceptions to this, see this short piece on mnemonics for academic learning: M. D. Miller (2012), Helping students memorize: Tips from cognitive science, *The Teaching Professor*, *97*(September), 1–6.

24. This is why retrieval practice is sometimes also referred to in the literature as the *testing effect*.

25. M. D. Miller (2009), What the science of cognition tells us about instructional technology, *Change: The Magazine of Higher Learning*, *41*, 71–74.

26. Great places to start include the books *Make it Stick: The Science of Successful Learning*, *Small Teaching: Everyday Lessons from the Science of Learning*, and *Powerful Teaching: Unleash the Science of Learning*, and the website www.retrievalpractice.org.

27. Classic articles on retrieval practice include M. A. McDaniel, H. L. Roediger, & K. B. McDermott (2007), Generalizing test-enhanced learning from the laboratory to the classroom, *Psychonomic Bulletin and Review*, *14*(2), 200–206, https://doi .org/10.3758/BF03194052; J. D. Karpicke & H. L. Roediger (2008), The critical importance of retrieval for learning, *Science*, *319*, 966–968, https://doi.org/10.1126/science.1152408; J. D. Karpicke (2012), Retrieval-Based Learning: Active Retrieval Promotes Meaningful Learning, *Current Directions in Psychological Science*, *21*(3), 157–163, https://doi.org

/10.1177/0963721412443552; H. L. Roediger & A. C. Butler (2011), The critical role of retrieval practice in long-term retention, *Trends in Cognitive Sciences*, *15*(1), 20–27, https://doi.org/10.1016/j.tics.2010.09.003.

28. M. A. McDaniel, H. L. Roediger, & K. B. McDermott (2007), Generalizing test-enhanced learning from the laboratory to the classroom, *Psychonomic Bulletin and Review*, *14*(2), 200–206, https://doi.org/10.3758/BF03194052; C. Wiklund-Hörnquist, B. Jonsson, & L. Nyberg (2014), Strengthening concept learning by repeated testing, *Scandinavian Journal of Psychology*, *55*(1), 10–16, https://doi.org/10.1111/sjop.12093.

29. For an in-depth discussion of different evidence-based study techniques, rank-ordered by effectiveness, see J. Dunlosky, K. A. Rawson, E. J. Marsh, M. J. Nathan, & D. T. Willingham (2013), Improving students' learning with effective learning techniques: Promising directions from cognitive and educational psychology, *Psychological Science in the Public Interest, Supplement*, *14*(1), 4–58, https://doi.org/10.1177/1529100612453266.

30. J. Siler & A. S. Benjamin (2019), Long-term inference and memory following retrieval practice, *Memory and Cognition, 48*, 645–654, https://doi.org/10.3758/s13421-019-00997-3.

31. A. A. Callender & M. A. McDaniel (2009), The limited benefits of rereading educational texts, *Contemporary Educational Psychology*, *34*(1), 30–41, https://doi.org/10.1016/j.cedpsych.2008.07.001.

32. J. D. Karpicke, A. C. Butler & H. L. Roediger (2009), Metacognitive strategies in student learning: Do students practise retrieval when they study on their own?, *Memory*, *17*(4), 471–479, https://doi.org/10.1080/09658210802647009.

33. A. S. Benjamin & H. Pashler (2015), The value of standardized testing: A perspective from cognitive psychology, *Policy Insights from the Behavioral and Brain Sciences*, *2*(1), 13–23, https://doi.org/10.1177/2372732215601116.

34. C. B. Kromann, M. L. Jensen, & C. Ringsted (2009), The effect of testing on skills learning, *Medical Education*, *43*(1), 21–27, https://doi.org/10.1111/j.1365-2923.2008.03245.x.

35. S. H. Kang, M. A. McDaniel, & H. Pashler (2011), Effects of testing on learning of functions, *Psychonomic Bulletin and Review*, *18*(5), 998–1005, https://doi.org/10.3758/s13423-011-0113-x.

36. S. C. Pan & T. C. Rickard (2018), Transfer of test-enhanced learning: Meta-analytic review and synthesis, *Psychological Bulletin*, https://doi.org/10.1037/bul0000151; A. C. Butler

(2010), Repeated testing produces superior transfer of learning relative to repeated studying, *Journal of Experimental Psychology: Learning, Memory, and Cognition, 36*(5), 1118–1133.

37. K. M. Arnold, & K. B. McDermott (2013), Test-potentiated learning: Distinguishing between direct and indirect effects of tests, *Journal of Experimental Psychology: Learning, Memory, & Cognition, 39*(3), 940–945, doi:10.1037/a0029199.

38. A. S. Benjamin & H. Pashler (2015), The value of standardized testing: A perspective from cognitive psychology, *Policy insights from the behavioral and brain sciences, 2*(1), 13–23, https://doi.org/10.1177/2372732215601116.

39. See, for example: The 47th PDK/Gallup Poll of the public's attitudes toward the public schools: Testing doesn't measure up for Americans (2015), *Phi Delta Kappan, 97*(1), 1.

40. A. C. Butler & H. L. Roediger (2007), Testing improves long-term retention in a simulated classroom setting, *European Journal of Cognitive Psychology, 19*(4–5), 514–527, https://doi.org/10.1080/09541440701326097; also see. A. McDaniel, H. L. Roediger, & K. B. McDermott (2007), Generalizing test-enhanced learning from the laboratory to the classroom, *Psychonomic Bulletin and Review, 14*(2), 200–206, https://doi.org/10.3758/BF03194052; H. L. Roediger & A. C. Butler (2011). The critical role of retrieval practice in long-term retention. *Trends in Cognitive Sciences, 15*(1), 20–27. https://doi.org/10.1016/j.tics.2010.09.003.

41. J. D. Karpicke & W. R. Aue (2015), The testing effect is alive and well with complex materials, *Educational Psychology Review, 27*(2), 317–326, https://doi.org/10.1007/s.

42. P. K. Agarwal, D'Antonio, H. L. Roediger, K. B. McDermott, & M. A. McDaniel (2014), Classroom-based programs of retrieval practice reduce middle school and high school students' test anxiety, *Journal of Applied Research in Memory and Cognition, 3*(3), 131–139, https://doi.org/10.1016/j.jarmac.2014.07.002.

43. J. Metcalfe & J. Xu (2016), Peoples' minds wander more during massed than spaced inductive learning, *Journal of Experimental Psychology: Learning, Memory, and Cognition, 42*, 978–984, http://dx.doi.org/10.1037/xlm0000216.

44. H. Sisti, A. Glass, & T. Shors (2007), Neurogenesis and the spacing effect: Learning over time enhances memory and the survival of new neurons, *Learning & Memory*, (732), 368–375, https://doi.org/10.1101/lm.488707.368.

45. N. J. Cepeda, H. Pashler, E, Vul, J. T. Wixted, & D. Rohrer (2006), Distributed practice in verbal recall tasks: A review and quantitative synthesis, *Psychological Bulletin, 132*, 354–380;

S. K. Carpenter, N. J. Cepeda, D. Rohrer, D., S. H. K. Kang, & H. Pashler (2012), Using spacing to enhance diverse forms of learning: Review of recent research and implications for instruction, *Educational Psychology Review*, *24*(3), 369–378, https://doi.org/10.1007/s10648-012-9205-z.

46. H. P. Bahrick & E. Phelps (1987), Retention of Spanish vocabulary over 8 years, *Journal of Experimental Psychology: Learning, Memory, and Cognition*, *13*(2), 344–349, https://doi .org/10.1037/0278-7393.13.2.344.

47. S. K. Carpenter, N. J. Cepeda, D. Rohrer, D., S. H. K. Kang, & H. Pashler (2012), Using spacing to enhance diverse forms of learning: Review of recent research and implications for instruction, *Educational Psychology Review*, *24*(3), 369–378, https://doi.org/10.1007/s10648-012-9205-z.

48. R. A. R. Gurung, & K. Burns (2019), Putting evidence-based claims to the test: A multi-site classroom study of retrieval practice and spaced practice, *Applied Cognitive Psychology*, *33*(5), 732–743, https://doi.org/10.1002/acp.3507.

49. M. D. Miller (2009), What the science of cognition tells us about instructional technology, *Change: The Magazine of Higher Learning*, *41*, 71–74.

50. www.kahoot.it

51. L. Zucker & A. Fisch (2019), Play and learning with KAHOOT!: Enhancing collaboration and engagement in grades 9–16 through digital games, *Journal of Language and Literacy Education*, *15*(1).

52. D. H. Iwamoto, J. Hargis, E. J. Taitano, & K. Vuong (2017), Analyzing the efficacy of the testing effect using Kahoot™ on student performance, *Turkish Online Journal of Distance Education*, *18*(2), 80–93.

53. N. R. Andzik, C. M. Gist, E. E. Smith, M. Xu, N. A. Neef, & T. O. State (2015), The effects of gaming on university student quiz performance, *Journal of Effective Teaching in Higher Education*, *2*(1), 109–119; K. Yabuno, E. Luong, & J. Shaffer, (2019), Comparison of traditional and gamified student response systems in an undergraduate human anatomy course, *HAPS Educator*, *23*(1), 29–36, https://doi.org/10.21692/haps .2019.001.

54. K. K. James & R. E. Mayer (2019), Learning a second language by playing a game, *Applied Cognitive Psychology*, *33*(4), 669–674, https://doi.org/10.1002/acp.3492.

55. R. Gafni, D. B. Achituv, & G. J. Rachmani (2017), Learning foreign languages using mobile applications, *Journal of Information Technology Education: Research*, *16*(1), 301–317,

https://doi.org/10.28945/3855; S. Loewen, D. Crowther, D. Isbell, DK. M. Kim, Z. Miller, Z., & H. Rawal (2019), Mobile-assisted language learning: A Duolingo case study, *ReCALL*, *31*(3), 293–311.

56. A. Grubišić, S. Stankov, & B. Žitko (2015), Adaptive courseware: A literature review, *Journal of Universal Computer Science*, *21*(9), 1168–1209, https://doi.org/10.3217/jucs-021-09-1168.

57. For more examples, see C. D. Dziuban, P. D. Moskal, J. Cassisi, & A. Fawcett (2016), Adaptive learning in psychology: Wayfinding in the digital age, *Journal of Asynchronous Learning Network*, *20*(3), 74–96.

58. https://oli.cmu.edu/.

59. J. A. Kulik & J. D. Fletcher (2016), Effectiveness of intelligent tutoring systems: A meta-analytic review, *Review of Educational Research*, *86*(1), 42–78, https://doi.org/10.3102/0034654315581420.

60. For example, see C. D. Dziuban, P. D. Moskal, J. Cassisi, & A. Fawcett (2016), Adaptive learning in psychology: Wayfinding in the digital age, *Journal of Asynchronous Learning Network*, *20*(3), 74–96.

61. P. J. Hughes (n.d.), Spaced learning to promote pharmacy student knowledge retention via mobile learning. Unpublished manuscript.

62. B. Sparrow, J. Liu, & D. M. Wegner (2011), Google effects on memory: Cognitive consequences of having information at our fingertips, *Science*, http://science.sciencemag.org/content/333/6043/776/tab-pdf.

63. Researchers in this study used an established methodology for demonstrating that a concept has been primed in our minds, even if we aren't consciously aware of it: the Stroop paradigm, in which we have to ignore a printed word in order to name the color the word is printed in. Concepts that we're actively thinking about tend to produce more interference, and slow people down more, than other words.

64. B. Sparrow, J. Liu, & D. M. Wegner (2011), Google effects on memory: Cognitive consequences of having information at our fingertips, *Science*, *333* (6043), 776–778. https://doi.org/10.1126/science.1207745, http://science.sciencemag.org/content/333/6043/776/tab-pdf.

65. D.L. Schacter (2022). Media, technology, and the sins of memory. *Memory, Mind & Media 1*, e1, 1–15. https://doi.org/10.1017/mem.2021.3

66. B. Storm (2021, July 16). *Cognitive offloading and memory in the digital age* [Conference presentation]. Cognitive Offloading Meeting 2021, Virtual conference.

67. For an example, see N. Carr (2008), Is Google making us stupid?, *The Atlantic*, July/August, http://www.theatlantic.com /magazine/archive/2008/07/is-google-making-us-stupid /306868/.

NOTES TO CHAPTER 4

1. Sperling wasn't the only researcher to employ this metaphor. Much earlier, William James talked about attention and spotlights as well.
2. G. Sperling & E. Weichselgartner (1995), Episodic theory of the dynamics of spatial attention, *Psychological Review, 102*(3), 503–532, https://doi.org/10.1037/0033-295X.102.3.503.
3. K. Cherry (2020, July 25), *How psychologists define attention,* Verywellmind, https://www.verywellmind.com/what-is -attention-2795009.
4. D. Griffith (1976), The attentional demands of mnemonic control processes, *Memory & Cognition, 4*(1), 103–108; D. G. MacKay (1987), *The organization of perception and action: a theory for language and other cognitive skills*, Springer-Verlag; D. G. MacKay & D. M. Burke (1990), Cognition and aging: A theory of new learning and the use of old connections, *in* T. M. Hess (Ed.), *Aging and cognition: Knowledge organization and utilization*, 213–263, https://doi.org/10.1016/S0166 -4115(08)60159-4; S. W. Tyler, P. T. Hertel, M. McCallum, & H. C. Ellis (1979), Cognitive effort and memory revisited, *Journal of Experimental Psychology: Human Learning and Memory, 5*(6), 607–617, https://doi.org/10.2466/pr0.1984.54.3.850.
5. F. I. Craik, R. Govoni, M. Naveh-Benjamin, & N. D. Anderson (1996), The effects of divided attention on encoding and retrieval processes in human memory, *Journal of Experimental Psychology: General, 125*(2), 159–180, https://doi.org/10 .1037/0096-3445.125.2.159.
6. N. L. Wood & N. Cowan (1995), The cocktail party phenomenon revisited: Attention and memory in the classic selective listening procedure of Cherry (1953), *Journal of Experimental Psychology: General, 124*(3), 243–262, https://doi .org/10.1037/0096-3445.124.3.243.
7. C. F. Chabris & D. Simons (2010), *The invisible gorilla: And other ways our intuitions deceive us*, Crown.
8. M. D. Miller (2014), *Minds online: Teaching effectively with technology*, Harvard University Press.
9. I want to credit Neil Bradbury, Professor of Physiology and

Biophysics at the School of Graduate and Postdoctoral studies at the Rosalind Franklin University of Science and Medicine, for doing the work to uncover the origins of the ten-minute rule. For an in-depth discussion of what he found, see this episode of the *Tea for Teaching* podcast: http://teaforteaching .com/16-student-attention-span/; or this article: N. A. Bradbury (2016), Attention span during lectures: 8 seconds, 10 minutes, or more?, *Advances in Physiology Education, 40*(4), 509–513, https://doi.org/10.1152/advan.00109.2016.

10. N. A. Bradbury (2016), Attention span during lectures: 8 seconds, 10 minutes, or more?, *Advances in Physiology Education*, *40*(4), 509–513, https://doi.org/10.1152/advan .00109.2016.

11. See, for example, https://business.linkedin.com/marketing -solutions/blog/best-practices-content-marketing/2016 /the-great-goldfish-attention-span-myth—and-why-its-killing -cont.

12. N. A. Bradbury (2016), Attention span during lectures: 8 seconds, 10 minutes, or more? *Advances in Physiology Education*, *40*(4), 509–513, https://doi.org/10.1152/advan.00109.2016.

13. A. E. Maynard, K. Subrahmanyam, & P. M. Greenfield (2011), Technology and the development of intelligence: From the loom to the computer, *in* R. J. Sternberg & D. D. Preiss (Eds.), *Intelligence and technology: The impact of tools on the nature and development of human abilities* (pp. 29–53), Routledge,

14. https://lindastone.net/about/continuous-partial-attention/.

15. Slack is a messaging and discussion application that's designed especially for workplaces.

16. A. Michel (2016, January 29), Burnout and the brain, *APA Observer,* http://www.psychologicalscience.org/index.php /publications/observer/2016/february-16/burnout-and-the -brain.html.

17. H. C. Woods & H. Scott (2016), #Sleepyteens: Social media use in adolescence is associated with poor sleep quality, anxiety, depression and low self-esteem, *Journal of Adolescence*, *51*(October 2017), 41–49, https://doi.org/10.1016/j .adolescence.2016.05.008.

18. H. Scott & H. C. Woods (2018), Fear of missing out and sleep: Cognitive behavioural factors in adolescents' nighttime social media use, *Journal of Adolescence*, *68*, 61–65, https://doi.org /10.1016/j.adolescence.2018.07.009.

19. See, for example, T. Tokuhama-Espinosa (2018), *Neuromyths: Debunking false ideas about the brain*, W.W. Norton & Co.

20. For examples, see David Strayer's work on cell phones and

driving; the influential theorist Alan Baddeley also has related how he was able to process certain kinds of input while driving, while others—such as visualizing the spatial arrangements of players in a soccer match he was listening to—interfered with each other: A. Baddeley (2003), Working memory and language: An overview, *Journal of Communication Disorders*, *36*(3), 189–208, https://doi.org/10.1016/S0021-9924(03)00019-4.

21. L. M. Carrier, L. D. Rosen, N. A. Cheever, & A. F. Lim (2015), Causes, effects, and practicalities of everyday multitasking. *Developmental Review*, *35*, 64–78, https://doi.org/10.1016/j.dr.2014.12.005; H. Pashler (2000), Task switching and multitask performance. *Control of Cognitive Processes: Attention and Performance XVIII*, 277–307; D. D. Salvucci, N. A. Taatgen, & J. Borst (2009), Toward a unified theory of the multitasking continuum: From concurrent performance to task switching, interruption, and resumption, *Human Factors in Computing Systems: CHI 2009 Conference Proceedings*, 1819–1828, https://doi.org/10.1145/1518701.1518981.

22. For another good discussion of task switching versus true multitasking, see P. A. Kirschner & P. De Bruyckere (2017), The myths of the digital native and the multitasker, *Teaching and Teacher Education*, *67*, 135–142, https://doi.org/10.1016/j.tate.2017.06.001.

23. Holbrook & Dismukes, 2005, as cited in K. A. Finstad, M. Bink, M. McDaniel, & G. O. Einstein (2006), Breaks and task switches in prospective memory, *Applied Cognitive Psychology*, *20*(5), 705–712, https://doi.org/10.1002/acp.1223.

24. R. K. Dismukes (2012), Prospective memory in workplace and everyday situations, *Current Directions in Psychological Science*, https://doi.org/10.1177/0963721412447621.

25. D. Diamond (2016, June 20), An epidemic of children dying in hot cars: A tragedy that can be prevented, *The Conversation*.

26. C. Cuttler & P. Graf (2007), Sub-clinical compulsive checkers' prospective memory is impaired, *Journal of Anxiety Disorders*, *21*(3), 338–352, https://doi.org/10.1016/j.janxdis.2006.06.001.

27. A. Gawande (2014), *The checklist manifesto: How to get things right*, Penguin.

28. See, for example, Donald Norman's 1993 book *Things that make us smart* (Diversion Books).

29. J. M. Lang (2020), *Distracted: Why students can't focus and what you can do about it*, Basic Books.

30. J. M. Lang (2020), *Distracted: Why students can't focus and what you can do about it*, Basic Books.

31. M. D. Miller, J. J. Doherty, N. Butler & W. Coull (2020), Changing counterproductive beliefs about attention, memory, and multitasking: Impacts of a brief, fully online module, *Applied Cognitive Psychology, 34*, 710–723.

32. R. Junco (2012), Too much face and not enough books: The relationship between multiple indices of Facebook use and academic performance, *Computers in Human Behavior, 28*(1), 187–198, https://doi.org/10.1016/j.chb.2011.08.026.

33. R. Junco (2012), In-class multitasking and academic performance, *Computers in Human Behavior, 28*(6), 2236–2243, https://doi.org/10.1016/j.chb.2012.06.031.

34. For an example of the concept in the education literature, see D. G. Oblinger, J. L. Oblinger, & J. K. Lippincott (2005), *Educating the Net Generation*. EDUCAUSE.

35. M. D. Miller (2015, June 26), Can millennials pay attention to classwork while texting, tweeting and being on Facebook?, *The Conversation*, https://theconversation.com/can -millennials-pay-attention-to-classwork-while-texting -tweeting-and-being-on-facebook-43100.

36. See, for example: P. A. Kirschner & P. De Bruyckere (2017), The myths of the digital native and the multitasker, *Teaching and Teacher Education, 67*, 135–142, https://doi.org/10.1016/j .tate.2017.06.001; A. Koutropoulos (2011), Digital natives: Ten years after, *MERLOT Journal of Online Learning and Teaching, 7*(4), 525–538.

37. D. T. Willingham (2015, January 20), Smartphones don't make us dumb, *The New York Times*.

38. B. D. T. Willingham (2010), Have technology and multitasking rewired how students learn?, 23–29.

39. K. Subrahmanyam, M. Michikyan, C. Clemmons, R. Carrillo, Y. T. Uhls, & P. M. Greenfield (2013), Learning from paper, learning from screens: Impact of screen reading and multitasking conditions on reading and writing among college students, *International Journal of Cyber Behavior, Psychology and Learning, 3*(4), 1–27, https://doi.org/10.4018/ijcbpl .2013100101.

40. M. J. Berry & A. Westfall (2017), Dial D for Distraction : The making and breaking of cell phone policies in the college classroom, *College Teaching, 63*(2), 62–71, https://doi.org/10 .1080/87567555.2015.1005040.

41. M. D. Miller (2017, December 8), Addiction, accommodation, and better solutions to the laptop problem, https://www .michellemillerphd.com/addiction-accommodation-and-better -solutions-to-the-laptop-problem/; R. Talbert, R. (2017, August

14), Laptop bans and the assumptions we make. http://rtalbert .org/laptop-bans-and-assumptions/.

42. A. Lepp, A., Barkley, A. C. Karpinski, & S. Singh (2019), College students' multitasking behavior in online versus face-to-face courses. *SAGE Open*, *9*(1), https://doi.org/10.1177 /2158244018824505.

43. John Doherty, to whom I'm eternally grateful.

44. R. Wiseman [Quirkology] (2012), Colour changing card trick, https://www.youtube.com/watch?v=v3iPrBrGSJM.

45. R. A. Rensink, J. Kevin O'Regan, & J. J. Clark (2000). On the failure to detect changes in scenes across brief interruptions, *Visual Cognition*, *7*(1–3), 127–145, https://doi .org/10.1080/135062800394720.

46. RYDBELGIUM (2012), The impossible texting & driving test.

47. L. Festinger (1957), *A theory of cognitive dissonance*, Stanford University Press.

48. E.g., J. Stone, E. Aronson, A. L. Crain, M. P. Winslow, & C. B. Fried (1994), Inducing hypocrisy as a means of encouraging young adults to use condoms, *Personality and Social Psychology Bulletin*, *20*(1), 116–128.

49. M. D. Miller, J. J. Doherty, N. M. Butler, & W. G. Coull (2020), Changing counterproductive beliefs about attention, memory, and multitasking: Impacts of a brief, fully online module, *Applied Cognitive Psychology*, *34*(3), 710–723, https://doi.org /10.1002/acp.3662.

50. C. I. Seymour, E. Erdynast, & M. D. Miller (2020), Gender predicts beliefs and knowledge about attention among college students, *College Teaching*, DOI: 10.1080/87567555.2020 .1853026.

51. https://pocketpoints.com/.

NOTES TO CHAPTER 5

1. H. H. Wilmer, H. H., L. E. Sherman, L. E., & J. M. Chein, J. M. (2017), Smartphones and cognition: A review of research exploring the links between mobile technology habits and cognitive functioning, *Frontiers in Psychology*, https://doi.org /10.3389/fpsyg.2017.00605, p. 2.

2. S. Andrews, D. A. Ellis, H. Shaw, & L. Piwek (2015), Beyond self-report: Tools to compare estimated and real-world smartphone use, *PLoS ONE*, *10*(10), 1–9, https://doi.org/10.1371/journal .pone.0139004.

3. P. A. Leynes, J. Flynn, & B. A. Mok (2018), Event-related potential measures of smartphone distraction, *Cyberpsychology*,

Behavior, and Social Networking, 21(4), 248–253, https://doi
.org/10.1089/cyber.2017.0630.

4. N. Barr, G. Pennycook, J. A. Stolz, & J. A. Fugelsang (2015), The
    brain in your pocket: Evidence that Smartphones are used to
    supplant thinking, *Computers in Human Behavior, 48*. https://
    doi.org/10.1016/j.chb.2015.02.029.

5. For a discussion of the right answer, and why it's so hard for
    people to hit on that right answer, see https://www
    .psychologicalscience.org/publications/observer/obsonline/a
    -new-twist-on-a-classic-puzzle.html.

6. U. Lyngs (2017), "It's more fun with my phone": A replication
    study of cell phone presence and task performance, *Conference
    on Human Factors in Computing Systems—Proceedings, Part
    F127655*, 136–141, https://doi.org/10.1145/3027063
    .3048418; Bianchi, P. (2018), *The Mere Presence Effect:
    Attentional Bias Promoted by Smartphone Presence*, San Jose
    State University. However, note that one other study did
    replicate the effect, using participants' own phones and a
    different set of tasks involving memory and attention: A. F.
    Ward, K. Duke, A. Gneezy, & M. W. Bos (2017), Brain drain:
    The mere presence of one's own smartphone reduces available
    cognitive capacity, *Journal of the Association for Consumer
    Research, 2*(2), 140–154, https://doi.org/10.1086/691462.

7. U. Lyngs (2017), "It's more fun with my phone": A replication
    study of cell phone presence and task performance, *Conference
    on Human Factors in Computing Systems—Proceedings, Part
    F127655*, 136–141, https://doi.org/10.1145/3027063
    .3048418; Bianchi, P. (2018), *The mere presence effect:
    Attentional bias promoted by smartphone presence*, San Jose State
    University.

8. B. Sparrow, J. Liu, & M. Wegner (2011), Google effects on
    memory: Cognitive consequences of having information at our
    fingerprints, *Science, 333*, 776–778.

9. Memorial Church, a popular site for architectural tours on the
    Stanford University campus.

10. L. A. Henkel (2014), Point-and-shoot memories: The
    influence of taking photos on memory for a museum
    tour, *Psychological Science, 25*(2), 396–402, https://doi.org
    /10.1177/0956797613504438.

11. G. E. Burnett & K. Lee (2005), The effect of vehicle navigation
    systems on the formation of cognitive maps, *Traffic and
    Transport Psychology*, https://doi.org/10.1016/b978
    -008044379-9/50188-6.

12. L. Hejtmánek, I. Oravcová, J. Motýl, J. Horáček, & I. Fajnerová (2018), Spatial knowledge impairment after GPS guided navigation: Eye-tracking study in a virtual town, *International Journal of Human Computer Studies*, *116*, 15–24, https://doi.org/10.1016/j.ijhcs.2018.04.006.

13. L. Hejtmánek, I. Oravcová, J. Motýl, J. Horáček, & I. Fajnerová (2018), Spatial knowledge impairment after GPS guided navigation: Eye-tracking study in a virtual town, *International Journal of Human Computer Studies*, *116*, 15–24, https://doi.org/10.1016/j.ijhcs.2018.04.006.

14. S. Dynarski (2017, November 22), Laptops are great. But not during a lecture or a meeting, *The New York Times*; D. Rosenblum (2017, January 2), Leave your laptops at the door to my classroom, *The New York Times*; Senior, J. (2015, July 9), The case against laptops in the classroom, *The New Yorker*.

15. K. Gannon (2016, May 15), Let's ban the classroom technology ban, https://thetattooedprof.com/2016/05/15/lets-ban-the-classroom-technology-ban/; R. Godden & A.-M. Womack (2016, May 12), Making disability part of the conversation: Combatting inaccessible spaces and logics, *Hybrid Pedagogy*, https://hybridpedagogy.org/making-disability-part-of-the-conversation/; M. D. Miller (2017, December 8), Addiction, accommodation, and better solutions to the laptop problem, https://www.michellemillerphd.com/addiction-accommodation-and-better-solutions-to-the-laptop-problem/; R. Talbert (2017, August 14), Laptop bans and the assumptions we make, https://guides.himmelfarb.gwu.edu/APA/blogpost.

16. H. L. Urry, C. S. Crittle, V. A. Floerke, M. Z. Leonard, C. S. Perry III, N. Akdilek, E. R. Albert, A. J. Block, C. Ackerley Bollinger, E. M. Bowers, R. S. Brody, K. C. Burk, A. Burnstein, A. K. Chan, P. C. Chan, L. J. Chang, E. Chen, C. P. Chiarawongse, G. Chin, & K. Chin (2021), Don't ditch the laptop just yet: A direct replication of Mueller and Oppenheimer's (2014) study 1 plus mini-meta-analyses across similar studies, *Psychological Science*, *32*(3), 326–339, p. 327, https://doi.org/10.1177/0956797620965541.

17. I wrote about this replication soon after it was published in the following blog post, which was also the basis for many of the same ideas I'm writing about in this section: https://www.michellemillerphd.com/a-new-replication-study-revives-the-question-is-taking-notes-by-hand-really-better-for-students/.

18. K. Morehead, J. Dunlosky, & K. A. Rawson (2019), How much

mightier is the pen than the keyboard for note-taking? A replication and extension of Mueller and Oppenheimer (2014), *Educational Psychology Review*, https://doi.org/10.1007/s10648 -019-09468-2.

19. H. L. Urry, C. S. Crittle, V. A. Floerke, M. Z. Leonard, C. S. Perry III, N. Akdilek, E. R. Albert, A. J. Block, C. Ackerley Bollinger, E. M. Bowers, R. S. Brody, K. C. Burk, A. Burnstein, A. K. Chan, P. C. Chan, L. J. Chang, E. Chen, C. P. Chiarawongse, G. Chin, & K. Chin (2021), Don't ditch the laptop just yet: A direct replication of Mueller and Oppenheimer's (2014) study 1 plus mini-meta-analyses across similar studies, *Psychological Science*, *32*(3), 326–339, https://doi.org/10.1177/0956797620965541.

20. H. L. Urry, C. S. Crittle, V. A. Floerke, M. Z. Leonard, C. S. Perry III, N. Akdilek, E. R. Albert, A. J. Block, C. Ackerley Bollinger, E. M. Bowers, R. S. Brody, K. C. Burk, A. Burnstein, A. K. Chan, P. C. Chan, L. J. Chang, E. Chen, C. P. Chiarawongse, G. Chin, & K. Chin (2021), Don't ditch the laptop just yet: A direct replication of Mueller and Oppenheimer's (2014) study 1 plus mini-meta-analyses across similar studies, *Psychological Science*, *32*(3), 326–339, https://doi.org/10.1177/0956797620965541.

21. To take one example, the author Evy Poumpouras claims in one recent book that as a graduate student, she hand-copied her textbooks word for word as a study strategy, explaining that this worked for her because handwriting is a research-supported way to make information memorable. Note that by copying word for word, she would have been missing out on the exact benefit that Mueller and Oppenheimer attribute to writing by hand—namely, that it forces us to synthesize and condense as we go along instead of transcribing verbatim. E. Pompouras (2020), *Becoming bulletproof: Protect yourself, read people, influence situations, and live fearlessly*, Atria Books.

22. F. Sana, T. Weston & N. J. Cepeda (2013), Laptop multitasking hinders classroom learning for both users and nearby peers, *Computers & Education*, *62*, 24–31, https://doi.org/10.1016/j .compedu.2012.10.003.

23. R. Talbert (2017, August 14), Laptop bans and the assumptions we make, https://rtalbert.org/laptop-bans-and-assumptions/.

24. S. Freeman, S. L. Eddy, M. McDonough, M. K. Smith, N. Okoroafor, H. Jordt, & M. P. Wenderoth (2014), Active learning increases student performance in science, engineering, and mathematics, *Proceedings of the National Academy of Sciences of the United States of America*, *111*(23), 8410–8415, https://doi .org/10.1073/pnas.1319030111; E. Mazur (2009), Farewell, Lecture?, *Science*, *323*, 50–51.

25. J. M. Lang (2020), *Distracted: Why students can't focus and what you can do about it,* Basic Books.
26. J. M. Lang (2020), *Distracted: Why students can't focus and what you can do about it* (p. 18), Basic Books.

NOTES TO CONCLUSION

1. J.R. Finley, F. Naaz, & F.W. Goh (2018), *Memory and technology: How we use information in the brain and in the world.* Springer.
2. For an outstanding example, see B.K. Kirchoff, P.F. Delaney, M. Horton, & R. Dellinger-Johnston (2014), Optimizing learning of scientific category knowledge in the classroom: The case of plant identification. *CBE Life Sciences Education, 13*(3), 425–436. https://doi.org/10.1187/cbe.13-11-0224.
3. S. Jang, J. M. Vitale, R. W. Jyung, & J. B. Black (2017), Direct manipulation is better than passive viewing for learning anatomy in a three-dimensional virtual reality environment, *Computers and Education, 106,* 150–165, https://doi.org/10.1016/j.compedu.2016.12.009.
4. M. D. Miller, G. Castillo, N. Medoff, & G. Hardy (2021), *Immersive VR for organic chemistry: Impacts on performance and grades for first-generation and continuing-generation university students,* in press, *Innovative Higher Education.*

ACKNOWLEDGMENTS

—

Thanks go first to this book's editor James Lang, whose work has changed the course of history in higher education, very much for the better. I've been a fan of his writing since I was a flailing new faculty member devouring his *Chronicle of Higher Education* advice columns through many a desk-bound lunch break or poorly attended office hour. He has been an eloquent and tireless advocate for evidence-based teaching and the forward-thinking faculty mindset that goes along with it. His work has opened up a world of possibility for people like me: psychologists hoping to communicate what we know about learning to wider audiences, and hoping to promote more learning in the world along the way.

Through James Lang, I was able to meet Derek Krissoff, who gave this book a home and a path to existence. As director of West Virginia University Press, Derek's vision has been clear, powerful, and ambitious, and nowhere more so than in the Teaching and Learning in Higher Education series. It's a project whose time has come, and thanks to him, the work is making it out to the people who need it the most.

I am grateful to the many brilliant scholars who created the original research that supports so much of what I've said in this book. Jeffrey Karpicke, Henry Roediger III, Robert Bjork, Pooja Agarwal, Richard Mayer, Daniel Willingham, Daniel Simons, Mark McDaniel, John Dunlosky, Pam Mueller, Alan Baddeley, Jason Finley, Daniel Oppenheimer, Kayla Morehouse—these are but a few of the researchers whose work has shaped our modern understanding of how people learn and remember. Any misinterpretations or misapplications of their findings in this book are my responsibility alone.

I was fortunate to have had the assistance of a team of NAU student researchers who helped with many key stages of this project: Dejah Yansen, Esmé Erdynast, Larissa Griefenberg, Zackary Sinex, and Caitlyn Seymour. These whip-smart and ferociously hardworking undergraduates helped ferret out relevant studies, surveyed the landscape of popular commentary about the topic, and offered insights about learning and technology from a twenty-something student perspective. Caitlyn, Dejah, Larissa, Esmé, and Zack: This book is better for your efforts, and was a whole lot more fun to write with you all along for the ride. Thank you.

I also couldn't have written this book without the experience of getting to teach the Technology, Mind, and Brain course in all its many incarnations throughout the years. Students in these classes have offered creative, practical solutions to the dilemmas we all face in a technology-saturated world, and they have pushed me to consider research in this area from totally new perspectives. I especially want to thank students in my Spring 2021 cohort who offered detailed feedback on an earlier version of the manuscript: Casiah Gueyser, Scott Janetsky, Kennedy Lopez, Alyssa Neal, Simone Simmons, Madeline Snyder, Jessica Valencia, and Maxim Vinnikov.

The feedback I got from West Virginia Press' excellent team of peer reviewers also immensely improved this book. In particular, Regan Gurung's comments, springing from his deep expertise in the psychology of learning, helped me strengthen the scientific basis for my advice to teachers. This book also got a major boost from the feedback provided by an anonymous WVU Press reader. We academics kid around a lot about the grief we always seem to get from "Reviewer 2"—but in my case, that second review was nothing short of inspirational. Thank you.

My husband Rick McDonald also inspires me every day with his commitment to the grand mission of education, and through his day-in, day-out work with students of his own. As someone whose educational-technology visions often exceed her skills in executing said visions, I thank my lucky stars that I have my own instructional design consultant available 24/7—and an infinitely patient one at that. Rick, your work influences mine more than you know, and your support has kept me productive, motivated, and un-stuck for all the time it took to write this book.

It's traditional to apologize to your family in the acknowledgments section of a book like this, saying you're sorry for the late nights, "vacations" spent hunched over a laptop, and all the other preoccupations that go with the territory of being an author. But to be perfectly honest, this book was never a chore, imposition, or unwelcome diversion. I had a blast writing it, and a happy writer makes a happy home. So in lieu of apologies, let me just say thanks for giving me space when I needed it and knowing that in the end, this book would be another thing for us to celebrate, together.

This book might not exist, and surely wouldn't be as good, if not for the unflagging support and spot-on advice of my longtime friend and minimally compensated writing coach Gary Schoep. Gary, you pushed hard to get me to put more of my own personality in this work and cheered me along the long road to finishing it, especially during the isolating ordeal known as the year 2020. Brains plus brawn equals book!

I've had yet another cheering section through the course of writing this book: my Mastermind group. I've gained so much from watching your colossal talents in action, Masterminders, and every time we talk, I come away feeling a little more optimistic that I can, in fact, do the things that matter. I won't list you all by name, because as we all know, the first rule of Mastermind is what happens in Mastermind stays in Vegas. But you all know who you are, and please accept my deepest thanks for all of our discussions during our five-plus years together.

My professional network also includes an incredible group of women who've encouraged me through this project and so many others. Rebecca Campbell's laser-sharp mind and wit challenges me, always with good grace and humor, to get better at everything I do. Kristen Betts has been a wildly productive collaborator; she is the one who invited me into her top-flight research group to complete the international neuromyths study I talked about the early chapters of this book. Kristen—I'm perpetually in awe of your energy and grateful for your friendship. Angie Moline—a brilliant visual thinker if there ever was one—opened up alternative ways for a word-nerd like myself to illustrate complicated concepts and big ideas. Rachel Koch and I laughed, visioned, and plotted during discussions fueled by countless rounds of appetizers, and I always came away feeling energized to stop planning and start writing.

Thanks, everyone. Let's do it all again soon.

INDEX

———

TEACHING AND LEARNING IN HIGHER EDUCATION

Skim, Dive, Surface: Teaching Digital Reading
Jenae Cohn

Minding Bodies: How Physical Space, Sensation, and Movement
Affect Learning
Susan Hrach

Ungrading: Why Rating Students Undermines Learning (and
What to Do Instead)
Edited by Susan D. Blum

Radical Hope: A Teaching Manifesto
Kevin M. Gannon

Teaching about Race and Racism in the College Classroom: Notes
from a White Professor
Cyndi Kernahan

Intentional Tech: Principles to Guide the Use of Educational
Technology in College Teaching
Derek Bruff

Geeky Pedagogy: A Guide for Intellectuals, Introverts, and Nerds
Who Want to Be Effective Teachers
Jessamyn Neuhaus

How Humans Learn: The Science and Stories behind Effective
College Teaching
Joshua R. Eyler

Reach Everyone, Teach Everyone: Universal Design for Learning
in Higher Education
Thomas J. Tobin and Kirsten T. Behling

Teaching the Literature Survey Course: New Strategies for
College Faculty
Gwynn Dujardin, James M. Lang, and John A. Staunton

The Spark of Learning: Energizing the College Classroom with
the Science of Emotion
Sarah Rose Cavanagh